Praise for *Leadership Material*

"Diana Jones enables you to create a presence wherein others follow you without being asked, people support you with being influenced, and repute is manifest without being forced. *Leadership Material* is a tour de force for building and sustaining personal impact."

—Alan Weiss, Ph.D., author of *Million Dollar Consulting*, *Million Dollar Maverick*, and over sixty other books

"A deep dive into what great leadership means today! If you need to improve your effectiveness and influence at work, you can be confident that Diana Jones' challenging questions and sage advice work. Everything you need to know to become an exceptional leader is right here!"

—Marshall Goldsmith, Ph.D., Thinkers50 number-one leadership thinker worldwide

"In these chaotic and disruptive times much is said about leadership. Leadership in a successful organization is shared; it is not only the ultimate decision makers that need to lead in this fast-changing world, it is multiple layers in an organization. Never before has true and authentic leadership more important. Leadership is about people, experience, and relationships. Diana's book *Leadership Material* captures the simplicity of that well."

—Steve Tew, CEO, New Zealand Rugby

"Diana Jones understands that a leader is not just what they do but also who they are when they do it. Presence is an ephemeral concept. Diana is giving it form."

— Matt Church, founder Thought Leaders Global

"This insightful book turns leadership on its head and questions long-held assumptions. A refreshing perspective on contemporary teams and relationships, with novel practical strategies for more effective communication."

—Jenine Beekhuyzen, Ph.D., author and futurist; Founder & CEO, Tech Girls Movement

"Diana's is a rare voice in the world of organizational leadership. Her approach, honed through decades of working with senior leaders in both government and business, is completely refreshing. Powerful leadership is highly personal, and it requires not only that we front up 'as we are' but also that we are willing to share our insights, even our vulnerabilities. This is book is a must-read for any leader who understands that their most powerful organizational tools are the interpersonal relationships and interactions they promote and support."

—Franceska Banga, Order of New Zealand Merit, professional
company director; former CEO, New Zealand Venture Investment Fund

"Diana speaks a new language of leadership that is motivational. *Leadership Material* gets to the heart of people working together effectively and achieving results through brave conversations."

—Jane MacGeorge, manager, Nursing and Professional
Services, New Zealand Nurses Organization

"This is the book all leaders should read. Diana captures what leadership development is about—that each of us has things to learn as we navigate multiple drivers in complex situations. We are the ones responsible for being calm in crises, communicating the real picture, and staying in productive relationship with people. These are not techniques. Diana's findings that these capacities come to the fore when we integrate our personal, practical, and professional experiences describe precisely what I learned. I wish I'd had this book when I was a CEO."

—Dr. Maris O'Rourke, former Secretary for Education for New Zealand;
former director of education for the World Bank, published poet and writer

"In these volatile times, true leadership is one of the most critical factors to create profitable growth in companies, since true leaders can help their company grow regardless of the economic environment. Too many books on leadership remain at a superficial level. In her book, Diana gets some levels deeper. She takes the reader on a multidimensional journey to reflect on and to create executive presence, a prerequisite for being a real leader."

—Prof. Dr. Guido Quelle, managing partner, Mandat Consulting Group
(Mandat GmbH); author of *Profitable Growth* and fourteen other books;
first European member of the Million Dollar Consulting Hall of Fame

"What resonates with me about *Leadership Material* is its central element that effective leaders blend their personal experiences with their professional identity. I know that too often this aspect is underdone in our leadership teams. In my experience this is essential to being an authentic leader that people want to follow. The solid analysis, insights, stories, and the practice steps at the end of each chapter help leaders draw the insights that they need to build their own effectiveness."

—Geoff Dangerfield, former CEO of New Zealand
Transport Agency, independent director and consultant

"Creating a more powerful and influential executive presence is the differentiator for the most powerful leaders in the world, and Diana's book comes at the perfect time—when we are exhausted by the old paradigms of leadership and anticipate and welcome a more thoughtful, socially intelligent leader to take our organizations to new horizons."

—Libby Wagner, adviser to global CEOs, author of the Amazon best seller
The Influencing Option: The Art of Building a Profit Culture in Business

"A must-read for any leader of people—your life and their lives will benefit from Diana's approach."

—Kevin Tso, CEO, Victim Support New Zealand

"Diana coached me as I was preparing to assume a senior executive role in the Government of Canada. I saw immediate results in my ability to maintain companionable relationships in conflict situations. Her book reflects her coaching approach. I recommend Diana's book to executives who want to be highly productive through inspiring relationships. The examples she provides in each chapter illustrate common behaviors we see at the executive table that we can all learn from."

—Karen Robertson, executive, Government of Canada

"This is a terrific book that goes right to the heart of effective leadership. Diana takes the reader on a journey into the childhood sources of 'unproductive' adult behavior and presents developmental strategies that can be transformative for leaders. It's been a long time since I have read a book that so clearly and persuasively links personal and organizational leadership. This is a developmental gem that is highly relevant to leaders and those that support them, and I thoroughly recommend it."

—Pete Cammock, Ph.D., adjunct senior fellow, and former director of executive education, University of Canterbury; director of the Leadership Lab; author of *The Dance of Leadership* and *The Spirit of Leadership*

"'Executive presence' is usually seen as the aura or charisma that a leader projects in his or her workplace. Diana Jones has taken that idea and turned it inside out—and we are all for the better because of it. This book shows us that executive presence is not something you show but something you reflect by aligning your mind, heart, and guts. This is a powerful finding. As an organizational psychologist working with Fortune 500 business leaders, executive presence is one of the most frequent discussions I have with leaders. Diana's *Leadership Material* will help many of my clients be more successful in their roles."

—Richard Citrin, Ph.D., M.B.A., founder of Citrin Consulting, author of *The Resilience Advantage*

"Diana Jones hits the nail of challenges and opportunity for leadership on its head. Her new book tackles hard topics that can be uncomfortable to deal with but are game changers for any professional looking to optimize their influence and accelerate their success."

—Karen Post, international branding expert, author of *Brand Turnaround* and *Brain Tattoos*

"In her fascinating new book on the importance of an executive's presence in relationships with other people, Diana Jones addresses this critically important topic from myriad angles and perspectives, including the executive's childhood experiences, thought processes, and emotions. All of these hidden factors contribute to the executive's ability to generate sustainable positive results. Jones masterfully explains a wide range of the nuances involved in building effective business relationships at the executive level."

—Dan Coughlin, president of the Coughlin Company, owner of the Business Leadership Centre, corporate and career specialist

"As an expert on talent, I'm convinced that executive presence is the differentiator between those who will remain in midmanagement and those who will soar to the top. I've worked with leaders in companies such as Microsoft, General Motors, and the Greater Boston Food Bank and have seen firsthand the power of executive presence. Thankfully Diana Jones' book has come along just in time to help the next generation of leaders unlock their hidden potential and become magnetic leaders."

—Roberta Matuson, president of Matuson Consulting; author of
Suddenly in Charge, *Talent Magnetism*, and *The Magnetic Leader*

"The twenty-first-century leader needs to bring all sides of him/herself to their work. As Diana outlines in her book, their strengths lie not just in their credentials, work experience, or career trajectory, but also in how they think, learn, act, and behave based on their individual background and unique personality traits. When they bring the softer side of what makes them human into the workplace, they create tighter bonds with those they engage whether those they manage, those who manage them or their peers. And that results in increased employee satisfaction, increased productivity, and better retention. Diana's stance is a refreshing one designed to foster better leaders."

—Kelli Richards, CEO of the All Access Group LLC, strategic
consultant, author of the Amazon best seller *The Magic & Moxie of Apple*

"Diana Jones has created an amazing road map, loaded with strategies and tactics, to enable leaders to transform the success of their organizations. *Leadership Material* is the book and mindset you must embrace if you want your organization reaching higher levels you never thought possible."

—Chad Barr, president of the Chad Barr Group,
coauthor of *Million Dollar Web Presence*

"Leveraging technology and big data is one thing; mindfully connecting with peers and customers is another. Relationships are often the missing link to mutually profitable business alliances. Diana's practical book shows you how to identify and shift unproductive behaviors and truly connect with others. That's the holistic approach that creates healthier, more sustainable organizations."

—Lisa Nirell, strategic marketing adviser at EnergizeGrowth LLC,
FastCompany blogger, award-winning author of *The Mindful Marketer*

"There's a gap between where leaders are and where they want to be. This as an important book to help close that gap written by someone who has been on the front lines. This book has global applicability."

—Dave Gardner, management consultant, speaker, blogger, author of *Mass Customization*

"Diana's book is a must-read for leaders wanting to inspire, engage, and have others want to work with them. Her insights, knowledge, and real-life examples are immediately relatable. This book is an essential resource for leaders and aspiring leaders who want to blend their personal attributes with their professional capacities for best business results."

—Kim Wilkerson, consultant, coach, and speaker; coauthor with Alan Weiss of *The Language of Success*

"At last there is a holistic book on executive presence that goes far beyond body language, phrasing, and how to act. A true leader knows how to view and understand their personal experiences in a way that makes them stronger, and larger. Unfortunately, too many leaders looking for executive presence bury their past rather than understand the emotional impact their past has had on how they act and how they are seen. *Leadership Material* takes its readers to a deeper level of understanding so they can connect with the people they lead and develop an executive presence internally, externally, and in their DNA."

—Simma Lieberman, "The Inclusionist," diversity and inclusion culture strategist, author of *110 Ways to Champion Diversity and Build Inclusion*

"In 2005, when I founded the International Sociometry Training Network, Diana Jones was one of the first chosen to link people to like-minded fields. Her podcasts on effective leadership are evidence of her generosity as an international resource. She offers the field of social network analysis a perspective grounded in J. L. Moreno's broader view of 'all of mankind' rather than systems committed to the status quo. For years, I have held her in high esteem as a treasured colleague."

—Ann E. Hale, author of three books; past president of the American Association of Sociometry, Group Psychotherapy, and Psychodrama

Leadership Material

*How Personal Experience Shapes
Executive Presence*

Diana Jones

NICHOLAS BREALEY
PUBLISHING

BOSTON • LONDON

First published in the U.S.A. in 2017 by Nicholas Brealey Publishing

An Hachette company

22   21   20   19   18   17   1   2   3   4   5   6   7   8

Library of Congress Control Number: 2016056210

Hardcover ISBN 978-1-857-88688-7
Trade Paperback ISBN 978-1-857-88689-4
U.S. eBook ISBN 978-1-857-88690-0
U.K. eBook ISBN 978-1-857-88687-0

Printed and bound in the United States of America

Nicholas Brealey Publishing policy is to use papers that are natural, renewable, and recyclable products and made from wood grown in sustainable forests. The logging and manufacturing processes are expected to conform to the environmental regulations of the country of origin.

Nicholas Brealey Publishing   Nicholas Brealey Publishing
Carmelite House   Hachette Book Group
50 Victoria Embankment   53 State Street
London EC4Y 0DZ   Boston, MA 02109, U.S.A.
Tel: 020 3122 6000   Tel: (617) 523 3801

www.nicholasbrealey.com

To Billie, Tamai, and Kahukura for
being unreservedly in my heart

Acknowledgments

I HAVE HAD THE PRIVILEGE of working alongside many senior leaders and their teams throughout New Zealand for the past thirty years with the Executive Presence program and as leadership coach and adviser. Thank you, each and every one of you. You have been an unreserved source of trust, learning, and inspiration. Leading requires grit, courage, and determination. You all have this in bucketloads. The case studies in this book come from my work with you. To maintain confidentiality, I have assigned pseudonyms and altered circumstances.

I have been deftly guided through the dilemma's that arise when working with others' development; thank you, Lynette Clayton, Chris Hosking, Dr. Max Clayton, Ann Hale, and Dr. Gordon Hewitt. To my many peers within the Australian and Aotearoa New Zealand Psychodrama Association, I give my unreserved thanks. That our lives were our leadership material in our own professional development was never questioned.

Without the encouragement, wisdom, and helpful comments of my longtime colleagues, this book would have remained only a languishing possibility. Thank you to Jeanette Schollum, Glenis Levack, Dr. Stephen Billing, Franceska Banga, Carol Mattinson, Keith McGregor, Russell Ness, Richard Moss, Dr. Mike Ashby, Dr. Antony Williams, Dr. Kevin Franklin, Jill Patterson, Shahla Motadel, Dr. Maris O'Rourke, Joan Daniels, Cher Williscroft, Rollo Browne, Linda Blum, and Sandra Turner.

My business mentor, Alan Weiss, and his community have provided me with an endless source of expertise, inspiration, professional development, and pragmatic wisdom. Your endorsements of my work ensured this book's fruition. Special thanks to Mark Levy for encouraging me to express myself simply.

To my agent, John Willig of Literary Services, and editor, Alison Hankey from Nicholas Brealey, thank you for standing firmly beside me despite the oceans between us.

Thank you, David, my partner, my hero. When I faltered, you said, "Just do it," so I have.

Contents

Foreword

L EADERSHIP HAS BECOME A TOPIC that tends to put people to sleep, a soporific that suggests team dysfunction, resistance to change, comparisons to Steve Jobs, labels such as aggressive/recessive G4 blue, and a sweat tent in the forest. If there is a subject in business more overdone and less understood, I'm unaware of it.

Yet organizations and individuals spend billions a year on improving leadership with scant evidence of any dramatic ROI. We endure Volkswagen emission criminality and Wells Fargo phony account fraud. We watch countless tax dollars wasted by poorly led government agencies—all of us have grown old waiting in lines at the division of motor vehicles.

How is it that a topic we can't seem to let go of we fail to methodically improve, while depending on the latest magic self-help book or the occasional natural and great leader to magically emerge?

Watching all this for thirty years while consulting to Fortune 500 organizations globally, I've determined that most approaches fail to consider the human element. We mistake money for motivation and glad-handing for goals. We've missed the obvious: People perform best when doing what they love, are great at, and for which they are recognized. When you give an unhappy employee more money, you merely create a wealthier unhappy employee. Just observe the U.S. Postal Service if you doubt that fact.

There is a myth that people resist change, yet people are actually quite fungible. They change readily when traffic jams occur, are quick to embrace new technology, and rapidly make adjustments when such change is demonstrated to be in their self-interests. People are not expenses and machinery assets—it's the other way around, although you'd never know it observing how most organizations, for-profit and nonprofit, treat their people.

In this original book, Diana Jones demonstrates how to combine the tangible and the intangible, the hard skills with the soft, the people with the result. She uses her keen observational skills to dissect what works and what doesn't, and like any brilliant coach, adds her own intellectual property to what you may have thought was simple common sense. Common sense trumps "conventional wisdom" every time in my experience.

Her focus on language and communication is refreshing in an age that lacks nuance and inflection because of the flat technology most of us are forced to employ. She delves into behavioral underpinnings and then explains how to deal with them pragmatically and in the moment. Her approach is never academic, her tone never pedantic. She reminds me of one of my favorite CEO coaching clients, who had a Ph.D. in chemistry: He was a scientist and a strategist.

Use Diana's findings as your lodestone toward truly enlightened leadership, which will be, counterintuitively, far easier than any "model," outdoor experience, or journey over hot coals. She assumes you're not "damaged" and provides the skills and behaviors we all need to lead people toward their maximum effectiveness.

I'm never been sure about what "presence" means, but I am sure this book is a large part of the journey to great leadership, and that's presence enough.

Alan Weiss, Ph.D.
Author, *Million Dollar Maverick, Million Dollar Consulting*
and over sixty other books

Introduction

M ANY LEADERS AVOID WHAT THEY SEE as "the soft side" of organization life. That is, they love to strategize, problem-solve, and talk about resources, yet they hate dealing with people problems. They see relationships as messy, touchy-feely, and intangible. That's unfortunate, because knowing how to work well with people is the key to being inspiring and influential.

I wrote this book to help leaders simplify the complexity of organizational relationships and behavior. I want them to see that by being less fearful of the soft side—and by genuinely connecting with people—their personal influence and professional success will expand dramatically.

Let me tell you how I arrived at this approach and why I think it's so important. I had been hired to facilitate a group of experienced leaders drawn from different parts of the New Zealand public sector. They had been chosen after extensive assessment center profiling and 360-degree feedback—and each one of them was headed for the C-suite. The goal was to build strong collaborative peer relationships between New Zealand leaders by sharing challenges and giving one another feedback. In those days, a facilitator was someone who provided frameworks to help conversations, kept their own opinion out of the content, and commented on the group dynamics. We were to meet for half a day each month for a year.

Our group culture rapidly became interactive and collaborative. Someone would put an issue on the table, and everyone dived in, like hungry seagulls, to get a piece of the action. I sensed a problem, though. While the discussions were exemplary on strategy, the leaders avoided reflecting on their behavior and their impact on one another. I felt we were missing the mark, me included.

Several similar group initiatives were underway across New Zealand. Some facilitators chose to bring in specialists to speak on various topics. I didn't want this. Knowing the depth of experience in my group, I sensed my role was to help these leaders build their relationships. I wanted to help them shift from social interactions to work interactions. How could we—as a group—interact in ways to fulfill the group's purpose? I knew *feedback* wouldn't work on its own. Using such a technique in this setting would be unhelpful and come across as forced. The only way I knew from my own relationships was to focus on my observations and invite here-and-now interactions. As a systems thinker, I knew I would have many opportunities to do so.

In our third session, Grant arrived late. Grant led the finance and strategy group in one of New Zealand's large government agencies. I knew he was intellectually sharp and very able. He was also the youngest senior leader in his organization and in our group. He knocked on the door, began to enter, rolled his eyes, and ducked his head down. He then made a funny offhand comment and slunk into the room. On the surface, group members greeted Grant and smiled, waiting until he sat down before continuing. I had seen something else. I watched group members grimace, look down, and visibly withdraw from Grant's entry.

With this observation, everything crystallized. Immediately, I became aware of my real role in the group. I had not seen Grant and the group members act as their genuine selves; rather, I watched Grant perform the role of the *playful diverting joker*, and others respond as if they had to tolerate him. I recalled moments in our earlier sessions when some participants talked incessantly, dominated, or interrupted. Others were abrupt and abrasive, and one contributed only when invited. At such times, people would roll their eyes or flinch, yet everyone was being "nice." You know, they didn't want to say anything. They acted as if they didn't want to hurt anyone's feelings—as if it weren't their role to address unproductive behavior. Yet what was happening affected the culture of our group, especially the value each person might add.

I realized I had been waiting for a mandate to intervene. In that moment, I knew what this group wanted from me was my experience, help, and insight. I shifted from being a facilitator to leading as an *insightful resourceful coach*. All this occurred in milliseconds.

I decided to address the situation head-on because I knew everyone was conscious of what had just occurred, yet was acting as if it hadn't. Grant sat down. The group resumed their discussion as if nothing had happened. I felt the unspoken tension. Knowing everyone's development goals, I decided to question Grant and to do this with group members.

"Are you interested in your colleagues' responses to you as you came in?" I inquired.

"Yes. Sorry, everyone, I was late." Grant grimaced and laughed.

I continued, "I was thinking that it wasn't your lateness your colleagues responded to. It was something else. Are you still interested?" Grant was alert to hear more and agreed.

At that moment, I had three principles in mind. The first was that the relationships and interactions in any group are a system; if I intervene effectively in any moment, that will shift the system. The second was that by bringing awareness of the interactions into the here and now, people won't analyze or talk "about" what has happened; they will share their experience directly from their response to what occurred. This provides the whole group with information they can use to adjust their behavior if they want to. The third principle relates to "walking the talk." If we as leaders aren't prepared to engage genuinely with one another, how can we expect engagement from our staff, across the organization or with our customers?

I continued, "How about you choose two or three people you'd like to hear from?" He chose, then listened to their concerns.

> Leader 1: "I didn't mind that you were late. I just didn't like your comment. I felt disrespected."
>
> Leader 2: "I like being in a group with you. You're a funny guy. But when you came in today, you made a joke. That diverted us from our discussion to focus on you. I didn't like that."
>
> Leader 3: "I'm late sometimes, too. What I noticed was the way you slunk into the room, and I thought that was weird. I was distracted. We are all senior leaders here. I wondered why you would do that with us?"

Grant, to his enormous credit, thoughtfully took these comments in. "I hadn't realized. It's true; I do like having fun and fooling around. But I also want to be a taken seriously." Grant relaxed. He began listening and contributing from his experience. He let go of being the *diverting joker* and became a *thoughtful contributor*.

Seeing people rapidly shift from being disruptive to being productive is a powerful experience for peers. They see the immediate and positive impact of their contribution, and their respect for one another deepens. Such moments of intimacy draw people together. Intervening with peers is not about doing something wrong or being reprimanded; it is about peers sharing experience simply and genuinely. In doing so, group members deepen their connections with one another. The culture of this group shifted from being nice to one another to engaging genuinely through their relationships. Their interactions expanded, and their mutual influence increased.

This engagement was a professional turning point for me. In deciding to be "the leader," I saw my responsibility was not to keep the conversation going, but to shift the conversation. By learning how to interact within their relationships—to say what they really thought and felt—the group could then collaborate at a deeper level, having confidence to tackle more significant topics.

At this same time, I was in discussions with members of the government's Leadership Development Center. We noticed that some promoted to leadership roles lacked influence with their teams and in the conference room. Some lacked confidence, composure, or gravitas with senior leaders and staff, while others offended with their abrasiveness. Bosses wanted their leaders to inspire and influence others, to capture hearts and minds through authentic relationships. They wanted leaders who could shape and lead organization-wide initiatives, change cultures, and work collaboratively—who possessed the flexibility and judgment to behave appropriately in different settings. In essence, they wanted leaders able to work outside of their content expertise.

I could see that this required a new approach and that we would need to develop a new approach to learning, one which went beyond the "workshop" paradigm of teaching concepts, skills, and tools to changing behavior. The Leadership Development Center staff and I decided to use the term "executive presence" to denote leaders' capacity to influence and inspire through genuine relationships.

I knew from my own experience that true behavioral learning is highly personalized and occurs within a relationship system of trusted companions. Learning processes include reflective, participatory, and experiential approaches whereby leaders can

- Experience their here-and-now impact with peers and experience what works and what doesn't.
- Decide their new response, one that is from their genuine self
- Behave in challenging work situations in a manner that is genuine, rather than a constructed persona.
- Realize they, too, can intervene at key moments to create productive working environments.
- Know that their own lives and personal interactions are their most valuable leadership resources.

From that moment on, I let my professional roles of *facilitator* and *conversation framer* fall into the background. I no longer felt the need to follow some imaginary "interaction rule book" or have a mandate from group members to intervene. I accepted the responsibility to help leaders interact with each other in the here and now—to express their hearts and minds rather than behave in some artificial or outdated way. My new leadership role would now be as *companionable peer* and *insightful,* here and now *resourceful coach.*

As group members deepen their connections with one another, superficial social interaction gives way to conversations about getting work done. From that original group, everyone, including Grant, was soon in the C-suite in either federal government, local government, or the private sector in New Zealand. Each remains an influential, sought-after leader.

For leaders to inspire and influence others to engage productively, the real work is to function as peers *while* maintaining working relationships. Peers who interact as equals never behave as if they were superior or inferior to one another regardless of their structural relationship. Two things differentiate their contributions: their personal qualities and their different functions. Leaders who build trusting, two-way relationships with people's best interests at heart attract talent and inspire others to do their best.

At an organizational level, there is (1) the agenda and (2) what really is going on.

It's a mistake to think a designated title on a chart makes someone a leader. Leaders emerge when they provide direction in a compelling way and actively contribute toward achieving their goals. When that coincides with a title, people are relieved. When it doesn't, people are confused and frustrated.

Leadership is not a theoretical concept. By signing up as a leader, you have signaled your capacity to create positive futures for others. This means that dealing with people, relationships, and behavior comes with the territory. It also means that at some point in your career, you will probably respond to a situation in a completely inadequate way. This could derail you, or at least cause stress, angst, and sleepless nights. Your worst nightmare as a leader has occurred. This is normal, but it can take you by surprise.

The truth is that you already have within you everything needed to respond appropriately. Executive presence is highly personalized, and the experience of development is personal and mostly private. The core premise here is that there is nothing wrong with you. Shifting circumstances and context have revealed something in your relationships and behavior that you haven't learned yet, and these are working against you. All you have lost is your spontaneity, your capacity to respond relevantly, but trust that these can be regained.

The type of learning required in these circumstances is probably new to you. Executive presence is not about memorizing tools and techniques, although these can be helpful as short-term solutions. Having presence is about changing your behavior by integrating your emotional responses with your thinking and the actions you take. This process is holistic, irrational, and illogical. The good news is that you already have personal, easy-to-access sources for doing this—your earlier life experiences, together with your current relationships and interactions. This is your leadership material.

I hope to provide you with information, concepts, and examples to stimulate your imagination and inspire you to truly connect with those around you. By navigating the soft sides of your own life, you will discover your capacity to truly connect with others. This will help you become pragmatic, empathetic, and effective, as well as someone people want to work for.

Reading this book gives you at least five things:

- Keys to communicate simply and clearly so people know your vision, direction, and expectations
- An increased capacity for empathy and mutual relationships
- Confidence to have peer relationships regardless of authority structures
- The ability to choose how you respond in stressful situations
- Courage to speak in the here and now

Let your imagination run free and explore what is possible with your relationships. We will distinguish the behaviors that either take you toward success or pull you away from what you want to achieve.

Through these pages, I want to give you confidence in what is possible. You can let go of any need you might have to know everything. Realize that you already possess the resources to respond differently to those situations that stop you in your tracks. Moreover, the very things you might want to hide or forget will assist you in becoming your genuine self.

To help you make your relationships visible, I will share various concepts and practices from sociometry, the science of relationships. I identify criteria that create interpersonal connections and explain how distance and movement can be used as measures of *closeness* in relationships, and identify criteria that create interpersonal connections. I will show which behaviors are likely to antagonize others and which ones will draw them closer to you.

By reading this book and working through the practice sessions, you will improve your abilities to read people and produce results through your relationships. You will discover that you can become more influential and relevant as you inspire others and produce great results.

Chapter 1

The Demise of the Rational Leader

THIS CHAPTER DEBUNKS THE MYTH of the rational leader. The belief that being logical and rational is the only route to leadership has steered leaders' development in the wrong direction. It's time to redress the balance.

The long-held belief that successful leaders are rational is not true. What is true is most leaders are capable of being rational when appropriate. If rational decisions always worked, we would have solved the enduring world problems of poverty, violence, and sustainable living long ago. Leaders who only focus on technical skills will discover that these won't help them have essential conversations or manage difficult situations. Such tools and techniques don't cut the mustard in leading people; they are only part of the picture.

How do you become influential? What do people want from you at the leadership table? What are the qualities that ensure people are drawn to you? And how do you develop these?

People like the idea of a rational leader. The assumption that rationality is better than any other way of working devalues leaders' personal experiences. Why on earth would we do that? The rational leader values thinking, reasoning, and facts over all else. They believe feelings are soft and fluffy—immaterial at best and irritating at worst. By valorizing rational leaders, we fail to acknowledge that leaders are people, and leaders need people to get things done.

After working with hundreds of different teams, both high-performing teams and ones facing difficulties, I discovered many leaders have a blind spot. Astutely aware of their strengths, they were unaware of how they negatively impact others. I identified three distinct types of leaders:

1. Those who understand how they are perceived, both positively and negatively. These leaders possess the quality of executive presence. They are confident, influential, and know how to work effectively with others.

2. Those who focus on how they are perceived negatively. Leaders in this group, while competent, lack confidence and are often stressed. These leaders may be perceived positively by their staff and peers, yet they are too hard on themselves and ultimately lack presence. They downplay their good reputations and ruminate on their own feelings. They lose their focus on how they assist those around them.

3. Those who do not care how they are perceived. They have their way of doing things, which seems to work—for them at least. These leaders are perceived as technically able and hard on people.

People's perceptions of their leaders matter. You know you're on the right track when people come to you for help or seek your counsel and advice.

Executive presence ensures you stand out from the crowd. With executive presence, people are drawn to you and want to be influenced by you.

From my coaching practice, I have learned that

1. Navigating the soft side and people dilemmas are a leader's most time-consuming problems.

2. The experience people have of working with you is just as important as the results you produce—and largely determines the results.

3. Leaders gain confidence when they accept their fears and anxieties.

Executive presence encompasses at least five essential leadership qualities. These invisible qualities

- Define your identity as a leader.
- Determine your credibility.
- Establish your reputation.
- Shape the relationships you have.
- Reflect your authenticity.

Each one helps you produce highly visible results. As we will soon see in detail, if you

- Gain insight into what creates influence,
- Identify sticking points in your way,
- Discover the source of any ineffective behaviors,
- Develop the capacity to change your behavior,
- Are perceived and sought after as a leader,

your capacity to inspire and influence and have greater presence increases dramatically.

Emotions Matter

Have you ever been in a dysfunctional meeting? Have you met leaders who argue, shout, grandstand, sulk, and withdraw? How on earth could this be? Leaders in dysfunctional teams act as if they were kids back in the sandpit, tossing their toys and stalking away in anger or withdrawing hurt and bewildered. Once the meeting ends, cliques form, and you are either in or out. Established ground rules are forgotten or ignored.

I decided that the "toys in the sandpit" analogy was worth pursuing. After much exploration, I discovered a significant relationship between earlier life events and current leadership behavior.

CASE STUDY: KELLY

Kelly, an international company representative, was constantly in meetings with large numbers of people she had not met before and might not ever meet again. Whether it was in Beijing, Geneva, Seoul, or Paris, she hated it. This was an essential part of her job, yet she froze and felt wooden. Her thoughts after the meeting outshone her capacity to contribute in the moment. When Kelly said one of her goals for executive presence was *to improve her effectiveness in interactions with others through receiving direct/straight/honest feedback on how she was perceived*, I was puzzled. I don't work with leaders who *don't know* how they are perceived. With years of performance feedback and 360-degree assessments, being senior leaders and not knowing how they are perceived would be unwise at best and impossible at worst. Kelly recounted that she had asked several of her managers what she might do to improve her interactions, and each one had said, "You are doing well. There is nothing extra you need to develop." She didn't believe them, and had enrolled in the Executive Presence program I offered. Knowing the lack of reality in such feedback, and the angst at being brushed off by your boss, I decided to work with Kelly.

Entering the boardroom to meet Kelly, I was taken aback to see an impeccably presented executive, drumming her fingers on the table in apparent impatience. My immediate perception was that that behavior would put anyone off. I remained friendly.

As we talked in this initial meeting, I asked Kelly what her experience was when she was in groups. I noticed she looked down, went pale, and was silent. Her eyes filled with tears. I was aware of a shift in Kelly.

I noticed a shift from her talking thoughtfully with me, describing her situation, to being still, not moving, and tears welling up. I sensed she was recalling a specific moment. I was curious and decided to inquire. I wanted to inquire in a way that made her free to respond at a level of intimacy she chose. "Where are you right now?" I asked. Kelly remained still and silent. I guessed Kelly was recalling an incident. I continued speaking softly so Kelly would know I was alongside her. "How old are you right now? What are you remembering?" Kelly looked at me and began her story. She reached down and showed me how small she was. "About four," she said. She told me that her family had immigrated when she was a toddler. In her first year of school, she stood out. She was oddly dressed and had a funny accent. Some girls at her school were members of the "in crowd." Kelly stood on the fringes of groups and was not invited in. While years of elocution had helped her speak clearly, feelings of exclusion remained and dominated her interactions in meetings. Kelly admitted that she never truly felt entitled to join groups, a belief that was in direct conflict with her professional role. Kelly had a goal for herself: "for others to perceive me as open, approachable, and at ease and include me in conversations."

Our work together over several months in the Executive Presence program included in-the-moment responses from trusted group members; role training,[1] including identifying her *harsh self-critic*, and seeing herself from others perspectives.

Kelly reordered her self-perceptions. She reported that: "It is not that I'm doing anything differently; I just feel different doing it. Instead of wishing the situation to be different, I now initiate, introduce myself, and get involved.

---

[1] Role training is a learning technology with four phases: contracting, scene setting, enactment, and integration. Its conceptual underpinning is role theory, originated by Jacob Moreno in the 1940s. Dr. Max Clayton further developed and taught the method throughout Australia and New Zealand starting in 1972. Both Lynette Clayton and Dr. Max Clayton refined and applied Karen Horney's (1885–1952) three subsets of coping behavior, enabling in-situ assessments to be made. In this book the words *role* and *behavior* are used synonymously.

"The basic elements are still the same. There is me, there is the group, and there is the encounter. What has changed now is my attitude and frame of mind. Rather than measuring my success or feeling excluded, I have a different frame on meetings. I keep going. I smile. I am entitled to be there. I say something personal about what I bring to the group, I ask questions, and interact. I know I am entitled to be there and I no longer freeze. By altering a few things in the mosaic, the result is a completely different picture."

Kelly discovered that the positive responses to her new behaviors reinforced her new approach. Her manager commented that her "generosity of including others is infectious." Kelly helped set the agenda rather than sitting in meetings realizing she had missed the moment.

Understanding *why* people behave in certain ways is unimportant; the main thing is how you respond. With this in mind, there are three keys to influencing successful business outcomes:

- Be aware of your own response to others' behaviors.
- Know where your response originates.
- Understand your current impact on others.

Leaders with presence are aware of the likely emotional responses that others have to their actions and decisions. Their communication and interactions reflect this.

Having a capacity to be rational is important. By being rational, you can

- Distance yourself rather than being immersed in details.
- Remove yourself from the swirl of emotions.
- Make assessments and see options objectively.

Rationality enables you to weigh things up and accurately consider different options. However, it is only one part of the puzzle.

Without thoughtfulness and people engagement,
action generated from being rational is likely to
produce ineffective solutions.

Behavior has at least three components: thinking, feeling, and action. Generated from our relationships with others, feelings are the physiological litmus test of our experience and inform our thinking. But acting from our feelings alone leads to impulsivity. When our thinking informs the actions we take, we are more likely to respond appropriately. The third component, irrevocably intertwined with the other two, is the action we take in response to our thinking and feeling.

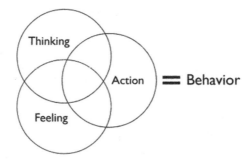

FIGURE 1.1   The Three Components of Behavior

Herein lies the problem. There are frequently two common misunderstandings made when praising rational leadership. The first is that considering the opposite of rational as "irrational," or "emotional," has diverted the discussion to discount some essential leadership capacities.

The second misleading element is that while some leadership theorists[2] identified emotions as significant, they may have misunderstood their function.

Rational leaders may well have the capacity to think analytically so that objectivity and logic come to the fore. But discounting feelings

---

[2] Weber, Freud.

and acting solely from rational thinking can result in others regarding them as cold and impersonal. Only a portion of their capacities are utilized. Their intuition, insight and foresight, and life experience have been excluded. I have found when leaders integrate their thinking, feeling, and action, people are affirmed, relationships are strengthened, and work progresses.

Champions of rational leadership emerged as management theorists of the 1920s. Henri Fayol (France) and Frederick Taylor (United States) saw authority vested in positions, not in personalities. In the same period, Max Weber (Germany) described three types of legitimate authority, one of which included the leader's personal qualities:

Traditional authority: arising from tradition and custom

Charismatic authority: where acceptance arises from loyalty to, and confidence in, the personal qualities of the ruler

Rational-legal authority: arising from the position of the person in authority and bounded by the rules and procedures of the organization

These theorists saw leaders within structured settings with prescribed roles. Results were achieved through leaders influencing the efforts of others with their ascribed authority. Emphasis was on structure, and leaders focused on what was "good for the firm."

Champions of rational leaders had at least two blind spots. They believed:

1. People follow orders. Stanley Milgram's famous experiment proved this while also revealing the anxieties, concerns, and fears of people who follow cruel directions.[3]
2. Organizational structures help people work together.

But this is not the full story. People are drawn to leaders with whom they want to

---

[3] Milgram, *Obedience to Authority.*

- Discuss problems.
- Share their thoughts and responses.
- Share how they feel about what is going on.

People want a sense of belonging and being valued; they want to influence what is happening whenever they are with others. Most organizational structures fail to account for this softer side of life, but leaders who can harness it can achieve profound results.

Good working relationships are essential for establishing executive presence. People with presence build positive mutual relationships, including with others they don't know well. These relationships are essential for producing results. Leaders do not need to have all the answers; what they do need is the capacity to adapt to shifting contexts and to keep relating to people around them.

Executive presence is not a skill or technique. Leaders with executive presence seamlessly blend personal experience with their professional identity. This enables them to respond relevantly to the myriad of people and events they encounter each day.

The Earth Is Flat—The Rational Leader Is Obsolete

All is not what it seems. Just as people once thought the earth was flat, many leaders still think that leaders' technical qualifications, objectivity, and rational decision making are the keys to producing results. I have another view—that qualifications, skills, and abilities are just one part of the puzzle.

That emotions have been part of organization life was reinforced by Max Weber, Sigmund Freud, and more recently Gianpiero Petriglieri,[4]

---

[4] Petriglieri, "Why We Pick Leaders with Deceptively Simple Answers." *Harvard Business Review*, May 9, 2016.

who said, "To distressed people in troubled times, the least rational leaders make the most sense." Eyal Winter[5] has shown that although "emotions are thought to be at odds with rationality, they are a key factor in rational decision making."

I agree that leaders' emotions are central to their functioning. And I bring another perspective: I have found that emotions are reflected in at least two factors that greatly influence leaders' capacities for presence and inspiration. These are:

1. How they work with people to get things done

2. How people around them experience working with them

Over the past three decades, much of my work with highly skilled and able leaders has focused on developing their capacities to integrate thinking, feeling, and action to create working teams and inspire others to action. They have done this through how they relate to others, rather than treating them as automatons who follow orders and do what they are told. Their work is to be "with" staff. They reject the notion of their staff "following"; rather they encourage staff to participate.

Two examples come to mind. One was in a federal bank where the leaders were all economists. The leaders directed the technical work; they used logic, reason, and numbers to make decisions and ignored leading people. Highly skilled and experienced staff, many also economists, were underutilized, bored, and frustrated.

The second example arose when I was contracted to advise on implementing a restructure in a city council.

CASE STUDY: FROM RATIONAL TO RELATIONAL IN A CITY COUNCIL LEADERSHIP TEAM

A group of ten leaders had re-formed, three from the original group and seven newly appointed. Four of these were from within the council and

---

[5] Winter, "Feeling Smart: Why Our Emotions Are More Rational than We Think." *Public Affairs*, 2014.

three from outside. While they barely know one another, their task was to lead a large department to manage the upcoming elections. Earlier events had caused staff to regard the leadership team as out-of-touch and irrelevant. How might this team develop their relationships rapidly to lead their department and deliver to the business? I decided to focus the first leadership meeting on developing connections. What became apparent was that there were many differences among group members; from the range of countries where they were born to their ages, their professional backgrounds, and their team functions. What worked well with this group was to build connections via what was important to them as leaders, their attitudes to risk, and their personal stories of life's turning points.

They decided *how* to work together by focusing on their staff. They rejected a wordy purpose statement and accepted "Staff feel inspired and supported to be the best in the department they love to be part of," and they made four commitments to one another:

- Make each department meeting meaningful, relevant, and enjoyable for all.
- Be open and transparent and ensure everybody has the information they need.
- Be a strong team, where we support each other and hold each other to account.
- Collectively commit to our individual leadership development.

Each leader chose two or three accountability buddies from within the group to review their progress. They held one another to account. They reported that their accountability meetings became professional highlights. The trust among the leaders and with their leader deepened.

Their business meetings became personable and frank and moved the business forward. They made every staff interaction a positive and personal interaction.

The problems identified, including performance problems, had shared ownership and were rapidly resolved. Within three months, staff reported that the department meetings were popular, affirming, and creative. The leaders engaged with one another with their purpose, and their staff engaged with them. They were logical and rational. Their monthly reporting of results engaged the other council departments.

Rather than being reserved and objective with one another, and sticking to their disparate functions, they committed to get to know one another and to emotionally engage. In doing so, their thinking, feeling, and action integrated, resulting in them working well together, and yes, the results they produced were "good for the firm."

Positive working experiences are essential for achieving results. Leaders may have all the technical and professional skills in the world, but if they rub their peers or staff the wrong way, this results in people moving away from them. They may even refuse to work with that leader. The leader's capacity to be effective grinds to a halt. Then the time-consuming and expensive work of repairing working relationships begins.

The rational approach to leadership led us to believe that our professional identity—such as leader, nurse, or worker—was the complete picture. But it is wrong to assume that professional identity alone is enough to compel people to listen to you. Would you respect the leader who disregards you, the nurse who is unable to listen, or the community worker who acts as if they are the boss and know exactly how things should be done every time?

If you favor the rational approach, you might be shocked to discover the leader has fudged the numbers, the nurse is highly anxious and makes mistakes with medication, and the community worker is out of their depth. Rational behavior is not synonymous with unethical behavior, but looking at personal qualities beyond the job title is essential to getting an accurate picture.

You can learn much about a leader by studying how they enact their professional identity. Enacting your professional identity generates five significant responses:

- How others perceive you
- The impact you have on others
- Your capacity to influence

- Your effectiveness in producing results
- The willingness of others to work with you

We know now from the demise of Enron, the global banking crisis, and many recent political downfalls that many revered, rational, and highly successful leaders snort cocaine, use company money for their personal lives, and lie to support their success. The rational approach fails to account for people's relationships and human frailties. We can learn from others that it is everyday interpersonal and group behavior that is central to leaders' producing results.

Houston, We Have a Problem . . .

On the one hand, we are independent, resourceful practitioners in specialized fields. On the other, we are embedded in social systems—whether we like it or not. We are leading people, not "things." Being a leader means you are likely to have many progressive behaviors; otherwise, you would not have attained your leadership role. Progressive behaviors are behaviors that

- Build relationships.
- Get work done.
- Produce enduring solutions to complex problems.
- Generate flexible, creative, original, and relevant solutions.
- Produce vitality in those involved in and affected by decisions.

Leaders' capabilities can be divided into two main categories:

1. Skills and abilities, such as financial management, project planning, strategic thinking, business analysis, and decision making
2. Qualities and capacities, such as listening; reliability; inclusiveness; and being forthright, fair, empathetic, and thoughtful

Experience and focused learning allows us to develop our skills and abilities as well as our personal qualities. This combination of capabilities is what creates trust. However, to achieve results we must be aware of our impact on those around us and maintain trusting relationships.

Our behavior—our responses to people and events—emerges from our experiences. The trial and error of life. As you progress in your career, you continue to encounter new experiences and new contexts. Some of your behaviors inevitably show up as problematic. These can become habitual. You may be aware of them or not, but they become apparent to others and affect the quality of your results. Your peers may sense you have more to offer.

Have you ever had the experience of coming out of a meeting thinking, Now that didn't go well? You might have had such anxiety over your performance that you lost sleep. If so, you have uncovered a default behavior.

CASE STUDIES

- Annie literally shakes with fear before going into the senior leadership team meeting. She rarely makes a comment unless invited.
- Ken smiles each time one of his executives disagrees with him or one another. He looks down and says nothing. Inside he freezes. He hates running meetings.
- "I don't like seeing that. Get it handled." Jeremy loses sleep over this comment his boss has made. He feels he has failed, again.
- Kirsty is the last to arrive in a meeting and apologizes profusely to everyone for being late. The meeting has yet to begin.
- Each time Rose comes to the C-suite meeting, she is argumentative and defensive. Usually collaborative and fun, here she feels she has to fight to be heard.

Everyone has certain behaviors they default to when they are under pressure. They become our way of coping with stressful situations. As we progress in our careers, work contexts change. When specific default behaviors become overdeveloped, problems occur. We might cut people out by letting our reactive thoughts, feelings, or actions dominate our responses.

Overdeveloped Behaviors Are Inflexible

Overdeveloped behaviors are obvious to others and frequently become roadblocks to our effectiveness. You *feel* you have no choice in how you respond, even if it is unhelpful, and others will notice that something isn't quite working. Generating choices at these moments is central to any leader who wants to develop executive presence.

Default behaviors often result from unresolved early family events where our survival was at risk. As children, we had few resources to handle the complex situations life threw at us. We did our best at the time, making different assessments and decisions depending on the circumstances—for example, "People in authority are stupid"; "No one is doing anything here, so I had better take charge"; or "The best thing right now is to become invisible." However, there is fallout. If those around you failed to discuss your experiences or comfort you, your childhood ways of thinking, feeling, and acting become entrenched.

We may have coped through such actions as going silent, taking control, giving up, or simply enduring. Feelings of shock, anger, or fright become entwined with our way of thinking and acting. Old memories and their associated feelings can be triggered by events and relationships in the present day.

It's as if you had returned to the original event, and you act as if you were in two places at the same time: then and now.

The Neuroscience of Behavior

Neuroscience gives us a way of understanding how the conscious and unconscious brain function, particularly with respect to our impulses and choices in organization life. The brain's limbic system is responsible for positive emotions, including tele[6] and empathy, and their linkage to memories of sounds, smells, and feelings. (We will return to this in chapter 3.) The amygdala manages survival impulses and our ability to move toward, be still, or move away from people with our flight, fight, and freeze responses. In contrast, the neocortex manages our curiosity to investigate different groups and to consciously choose to move toward or away from them.

Default responses governed by the limbic system come to the fore where people feel under threat. Leaders with weak connections between their self-awareness and self-management act as if they were back in the original pattern of events. Daniel Goleman coined the term *amygdala hijack* to describe situations when we behave inappropriately.[7] Amygdala hijack is a reflection of overdeveloped default behavior. Inappropriate responses are out of kilter and fail to progress the situation.

Leaders fall out of their leadership role and act as if they are somewhere else. They overreact as default behaviors kick in. There is nothing inherently wrong with this. Problems occurs when

- Your default behavior becomes your everyday response.
- The stress induced by your behavior interferes with your capacity to work well with others and produce results.
- You are unaware of how people are responding to you.

Recognizing similar patterns of behavior in early life can lead to insightful moments of self-discovery. For some, recognizing a connection is enough for them to break the link. Others require more work and must tap deeper into the personal dimension of professional development.

---

[6] 'Tele is the flow of feeling between people reflecting their emotional connection.'
[7] Goleman, *Emotional Intelligence*.

Behavioral change stimulates physiological changes and vice versa. Neurobiologists proved that attention to one's interpersonal world is directly connected to spiritual, emotional, and physical well-being.[8] We can shift from being stressed and reactive to being calm and responsive. The amygdala and the unconscious brain cede control to the conscious brain, and the neocortex takes the lead in managing our behavior. When thinking, feeling, and action are all aligned, there is a shift from flight, fright, or freeze to fascination and curiosity. Capacities for interpersonal engagement expand.

Originating events for default behaviors are diverse, but two themes are particularly common. One relates to the nature of structural or power relationships in organizations. The second relates to leaders' behavior within those relationships—being disinterested, absent, invasive, aggressive, or critical. People acting from default behaviors are typically unaware they are causing harm, and most would be horrified to know that was the case. One implication of this dynamic is that self-awareness and self-management are crucial for leaders.

Leaders with overdeveloped default behaviors often fall into traps such as

- Taking feedback as a personal attack.
- Responding aggressively, blaming, accusing, and being defensive.
- Losing confidence, having low self-esteem, and self-doubting.

They fall out of their peer relationships and act either superior or inferior to their colleagues. They create distance between themselves and those around them. People move away from leaders who are defensive, verbally abusive, or prone to blaming. Some leaders erect defensive barriers through excessive describing, explaining, or analyzing. Others effectively remove themselves by acquiescing and remaining silent on important matters. Leaders with self-doubt and low self-esteem rarely offer themselves for difficult and rewarding work. When events within the organization

---

[8] Seigal, *An Interpersonal Neurobiolgoy Approach to Psychotherapy*, 2006. Cited in Hale, *Three Cyclical Models Which Enhance Consciousness of Interpersonal Connections*, 2012.

mirror earlier experiences, leaders respond as if they were children back in early life.

There are four likely triggers for default behavior:

- The demeanor of one or more of the players
- The emotional tone of the setting, group, or meeting
- The experience of being hurt, ignored, or applauded
- A change in the structural relationship with staff, peers, authority figures, and siblings.

As triggers persist, default behaviors become overdeveloped. The situation may change, yet old default responses remain. Our capacity to choose how to respond has vanished. If leaders realize that a given habitual response no longer works well, they will have uncovered one of their overdeveloped default behaviors. They may fear that their managers, peers, and staff will doubt their abilities—a stressful thought. On top of this, they may doubt themselves and worry others will avoid working with them unless they have to.

Overdeveloped default behaviors are inflexible and unfit for the purpose of leadership. When leaders give power to their overdeveloped default behaviors, the same problems resurface over and over again. The relationships among their thinking, feeling and actions are out of sync.

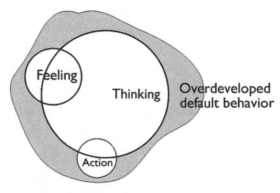

FIGURE 1.2   When Thinking Dominates Behavior

When leaders' thinking dominates their feeling and action, they might be perceived as conceptually or technically brilliant while lacking empathy or failing to produce results.

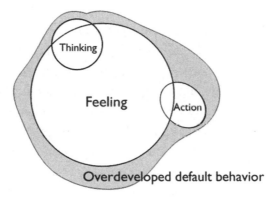

FIGURE 1.3 When Feelings Dominate Behavior

When feelings dominate leaders' interactions, decisions lack thought and are caught up in an emotional churn. They may be perceived as a poor "fit" with the work culture.

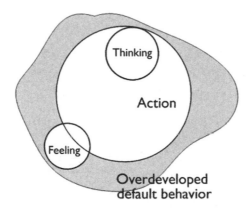

FIGURE 1.4 When Action Dominates Behavior

When actions dominate, leaders may be perceived as impulsive and unstrategic, jumping to solutions without foresight.

Progressive Behavior

With executive presence, leaders' thinking, feeling, and actions are integrated. Their behavior is progressive, meaning that they build relationships quickly and their contributions produce obvious value. Results are evident.

Progressive behavior is fit-for-purpose. This is evident in leadership teams where interactions are purposeful and engaging and business moves forward. Those around leaders who act from progressive behaviors recognize their vitality, flexibility, originality, and creativity. Leaders themselves discover that new responses are possible for what were previously triggering situations. They generate effective responses in new situations.

And now the complexity begins. An organization's purpose, structures, and defined roles all make good sense in a rational world. But organizations are made up of people in relationships with one another. Either they want to work together or they do not. An organization might have a great mission statement and a well-defined organization chart, with clear roles and responsibilities, but unless specific people are willing to work together, and work well together, the outcomes are likely to be dismal.

CASE STUDY:

Morrie's job was on the line. He was a seasoned adviser to senior executives. While he was technically brilliant, several executives complained to his boss he was rude and didn't listen. Two refused to work with him. Where did this come from? From the time he was seven, Morrie grew up in foster homes. He'd learned to survive by fighting for himself and for his companions. Whenever a senior leader made demands or disagreed with his advice, Morrie would speak loudly and authoritatively, not pausing for breath. Routinely, he would interject, "You are wrong."

Leaders with overdeveloped default behaviors are inflexible. Their behaviors are not fit for purpose. They create emotional churn around them. People might find them intellectually stunning but dislike working with them.

The Leader's Dilemma

How do you let people know their behavior is unacceptable? Alerting peers and staff of this is one of the most anxiety-inducing tasks for any leader. Whether you are performance managing or coaching, opening a conversation about the impact of someone's behavior requires courage. Everyone is aware that "something is not right here," that there is an elephant in the room. Whose job is it to raise the issue, and how do you describe what is happening? You awkwardly feel as if you *should* say something, yet pause, fearing you might break some invisible taboo. Once it is out there, some people are relieved, but others are shocked. Ideally, a conversation ensues.

Bringing development discussions into a relationship with a colleague or direct report is similar. If a colleague breaks team confidentiality or a staff member shouts when she is upset, raising the subject is not easy, but if leaders don't act, the tension will only escalate. If you find yourself worrying how to have this conversation, you have several options:

- Leave it and hope it will go away. Assume you are not the "right" person to raise it. *This only works if you know that it is not your mandate to intervene. Wasting emotional time and energy fretting is unhelpful. Trust your relationships, judgment, and intuition. Focus on what you can control.*

- Find a person who has a good working relationship with the problem boss or coworker. *Find out their perspective and share yours. Stand beside them psychologically as they take action. Contribute to forward movement.*

- Have the conversation. *If your heart isn't beating rapidly, then it's a good time to have the conversation. Share your observations, listen, then communicate what you expect. Arrive at a mutual understanding.*

Some leaders analyze "why" an employee behaves in a particular way, then they become concerned they are in the domain of therapy. They're not, but analyzing "why" won't help a leader to act. It takes them in wrong direction. Making an assessment of the impact of such behavior on results is the leader's terrain. Addressing unproductive behavior is definitely the leader's mandate as it is the quality of the leader-employee relationships that shapes the work culture.

Counterproductive behavior most likely stems from the earlier lives of executives, but the details of these matters are private. To have presence as a leader, it is wise to identify your own overdeveloped default behaviors. Establishing the connection between them and their historical origin is necessary, and applying these insights to your current context is essential. Having a vision for your refreshed personal qualities, aligned with your professional identity, is integral to your capacity for presence.

Shifting Default Behaviors

As a child, make no mistake, you did your best. You did not have the capacities—physically, socially, or emotionally—to respond to events as an adult would. You coped. Typically, those caring for you were unavailable or didn't assist you in the right way. Being isolated during significant traumatic childhood moments is the main source of current behavioral glitches. What was missing then was knowing that someone saw and knew what occurred, that someone cared for and *took care of* you. This can be as simple as physical comforting and mirroring: "You've been hurt" or "I'm here now. You thought we had forgotten you." The reality is that often this did not occur, which led to the development of self-protective survival behaviors.

Once default behaviors become apparent in our work, there are a wide range of people who can help. Trusted intimate friends, bosses, colleagues, and mentors can be a great source of understanding. For others, counseling or therapy are helpful to review and come to terms with the effects of originating events. Both approaches create a sense of freedom, of a weight being lifted. Your current responses become *in the moment.*

The key thing with a default response is that you are deprived of your ability to think. Realizing that this relates to the originating events, rather than your current situation, begins the process of repair. This sounds really serious, and for many, it is. It is also the stuff of everyday life. While others may be at "fault," taking responsibility for your work behavior begins with you. Know that you now have people alongside you who do care—about you personally and about all you have to offer; colleagues, partners, and friends.

I have discovered that leaders expand their executive presence by tapping into their own early life experiences. By doing so, they discover three things:

- The likely source of their overdeveloped defaults and coping responses
- Clues for fresh responses and progressive behaviors
- Greater capacities to maintain companionable relationships under stressful conditions

Leadership development can have therapeutic effects in at least three ways:

1. Executives realize other leaders share default behaviors, self-doubt, and poor confidence. They realize they are not alone.
2. The experience of trusted companions alongside looking into their situation without judgment gives confidence for acceptance and fresh possibilities.
3. Positive, functional, and progressive meetings where participants are heard and understood and where decisions are made that move the business forward and facilitate trust.

Who you undertake your professional development with is your choice. My best advice is to choose a trusted coach, trainer, counselor, mentor, friend, colleague, or boss who understands human behavior and has your best interests at heart. Choosing trusted confidants is essential to every leader's psychological well-being. (More details are found in chapter 2.)

Diving into the Wreck

I grew up in a war zone. My parents fought constantly. Both were the eldest of four. Dad was an engineer, funny, intelligent, and moody. Mum was an economist, gregarious, smart, and busy. Not wanting to be caught in the constant crossfire, I kept quiet during their fights. I made myself invisible and became silently critical of my parents. I dreamed of a better family life. We never discussed what was happening. My picture of a happy family didn't match my experience.

My parents' fighting had an unusual impact on me. Wherever I went, I saw possibilities. Outside of home, I spoke out. I was perceptive and articulate. Being chosen as a leader became second nature to me; I was captain of our school netball team, started my own PE class at college, and led a regional group of teachers discussing education reform as a first-year teacher. I sensed I had things to offer and shared my ideas. I gave status updates to those in authority. I continued to be given formal and informal leadership roles as someone who had vision. I would get a job and change things dramatically for the better. My reputation was one of being innovative and producing results. After several falling-outs with bosses and peers, I realized they didn't like working with me. I had become critical, task oriented, and unappreciative. The context had changed. My behavior and relationships were no longer fit-for-purpose. "I" had become invisible. I was behaving as if I was still in the war zone and didn't trust anyone around me. I decided to review my approach to leading others.

Discovering Early Influencers

When I work with leaders and their development, I first say, "Tell me a bit about your background." Many begin with some of the work roles they have had. Then they let me know about some of their family circumstances. Some say, "Do you mean personal or work?" I respond, "You decide." Most clients are willing to talk about their family background and encapsulate what they want to say in a few words.

CASE STUDY:

- Viv routinely takes on too much and is exhausted. I ask where she learned to do this. "My mother had depression, so my job was to look after my nine brothers and sisters."
- Gerry is overloaded from taking on too much. He complains about his manager not being interested in him. I ask him when he first became aware of this pattern. "From the time I was two, I lived in an orphanage. I hated it. The other kids really liked me, so I was a leader from early on. I was the one who saw what needed to happen."
- Harry drones on in leadership meetings and can't shift gears quickly enough. I ask where he learned to talk like this. He immediately responds, "I was the eldest of four. My dad died when I was twelve, and suddenly I was the family spokesperson."

When diving into any wreck, it is reassuring and helpful to have a mutually trusted companion. Solo journeys are possible, but personal resilience is essential.

By diving deep, you are searching for your genuine self.

When I work this way, clients appreciate I have a sense of the practicality of their current situation. I don't need to know the details of the originating experience, but they sense I am aware of its profound impacts. I use all my senses and remain aware of how their eye movements, breathing, and facial expressions might relate to their behavior. My background as a physical educator helps me assess physiology, movement, and posture. As a sociometrist, I am alert to behaviors that either isolate people or create connections. I apply all my knowledge, experience, and intuition to my working relationships. A client sharing a moment of insight, recognition, and acceptance is deeply personal to them and a professional privilege for me.

Diving into the wreck is not about finding the key, opening up boxes, and rummaging around. What works is identifying the particular earlier events linked to current unworkable default responses.

Recognition and acceptance, rather than denial and retreat, gives you freedom to choose. You have arrived at a moment of choice; you can either continue as usual or open yourself to other possibilities.

Choosing your response in stressful situations results in a clear flow of feeling between you and others. Interruptions in relationships and communication cease. The genuine you is present and you can connect easily with others. People are drawn to you and want to be influenced by you.

Practice Session 1.1

Rate yourself on a 1–10 scale for each of these criteria for executive presence, 0 being not at all, 10 being fit-for-purpose.

- You anticipate resolving people problems and maintaining good relationships.
- People look to you for context, decision making, and direction.
- You know what is going on in your organization.
- You contribute relevantly in groups.
- You are sought after for advice and counsel.
- You have a personal network of trusted advisers.
- You are calm in crises.
- You can disagree with others and maintain good relationships.
- You are less than perfect, and people accept you.
- You look forward to being with people.
- You can transact business rapidly.
- You are perceived as accessible, relevant, insightful, and results oriented.

Practice Session 1.2

What and who have been the four most powerful influences on you as a leader?

1. _____
2. _____
3. _____
4. _____

What did you learn from each one, and specifically what have they helped you do?

1. _____
2. _____
3. _____
4. _____

Practice Session 1.3

What are three overdeveloped default behaviors you currently have?

1. _____
2. _____
3. _____

Where did each of these come from?

Summary

- Develop executive presence by blending your personal experience with your professional identity.
- You don't need all the answers; what you do need is the capacity to relate relevantly to shifting contexts and to those around you.
- When you discover an overdeveloped default behavior, tap into your own early life experiences to uncover the likely source.

- The changes in behavior you might make are small; for example, you may speak more quietly or look people in the eye, yet they have significant impacts on results.
- Be aware that this professional development approach entails making significant emotional and psychological shifts.
- Hit the refresh button and update your responses to be appropriate to the settings you find yourself in.
- Rationality is a valuable characteristic for leaders with presence. Equally valuable is the ability to navigate the soft side of organizational life: people, relationships, and behavior.
- Your emotional responses are central to your capacities to lead and engage relevantly.
- Executive presence is deeply personal.

Chapter 2

How to Show Up in a Meaningful Way

IT IS A MYTH that a leader's personal qualities must remain separate from their professional identity. This chapter looks at the relationship between personal and professional qualities as they relate to executive presence. The key is that leaders with presence know how to differentiate and choose which elements of their personal self to share each day.

Working exclusively from their professional identity is unwise. Without actively choosing their personal qualities, leaders are seen as faceless bureaucrats. I've discovered the relationship between personal qualities and professional presence is precisely what creates your identity as a leader.

Personal and Professional Qualities— Differentiated, Not Separate

Many years ago, an event occurred that shook me to my core. This experience influenced how I show up in life.

Late one April night, I received a call. A colleague said that three of my dearest friends had died in a car accident. I couldn't think. I didn't want to believe it.

I was scheduled to lead a retreat with a leadership team two days later. I wanted to back away, cover myself with a blanket, and hide. I consulted my mentor. His wisdom stayed with me: "Hold your dear friends in your hand. Make a fist, place your fist below your collar bone, and hold your friends there. You can take them out again at the end of each day. What has happened and how you feel can remain private."

My personal self stabilized and moved into the background as my professional self came to the foreground, and I went ahead with the meeting. Unexpectedly, I sat for much of the time. There were moments I felt overwhelmed. I placed my hand above my heart and kept my inner thoughts and feelings private. The group and I worked very well and had a productive session. That evening, I shared my grief with a close friend.

In that moment, I reformed the relationship between my personal and professional identities. I learned to choose what I let come to the foreground in my interactions and that shaping my identity can be a conscious choice.

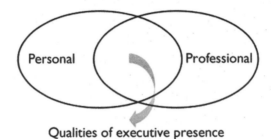

Qualities of executive presence

FIGURE 2.1   Choosing the Relationship between Personal and
Professional Identities

Up until then, I'd always been open about my personal responses to what was going on around me. Others liked this trait in me and the intensity it created, but I learned to differentiate further what to share while remaining purposeful in my work. I became aware of different degrees of intimacy for sharing my own feelings and experiences. I realized that I didn't have to share everything with everyone. In this setting, I was devastated but chose not to let the group know. I kept what had happened private and instead focused on the leaders and their work.

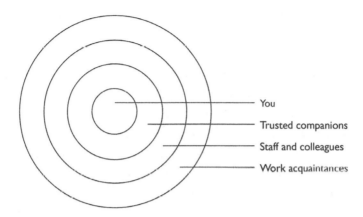

You

Trusted companions

Staff and colleagues

Work acquaintances

FIGURE 2.2   Leaders Thoughtfully Choose What They Share and with Whom

Our emotional responses are closely tied to our everyday interactions; of being with staff, customers, colleagues, and in large groups. How do we *manage* our emotional responses? By clarifying the relationship between your personal qualities and your professional identity, *you* can decide what shape your public identity will take. Choosing the qualities you bring to the fore enables you to function more effectively than if they were in the background.

The key here is to ensure that you, as leaders, do make that choice—and not be driven by your emotions or by your thinking. Leaders can choose what they share and with whom, as with any other relationships in life.

How Is Trust Created Among Leaders?

Leaders who barely know one another are expected to work well together and make business decisions. While trust and collaboration between the CEO and senior leaders are critical for success, both can be scarce. Interpersonal competition, frequently under the guise of disparate corporate functions, and behind-the-back criticism can be rife.

Trust is generated at an emotional level. Trusted relationships enable leaders to let others know their vulnerabilities, believing they won't take advantage and that the confidant has their best interests in mind. If specific actions to create trust among team members aren't taken, they will get by, but without their best efforts.

When you are a trusted leader, you can initiate the tough conversations, whether that is a development conversation with a staff member or pushing back on an unrealistic time frame with your CEO. What you offer is accepted as constructive. If you are not prepared to be vulnerable, you may not be able to develop the depth of trust for effective leadership. Being vulnerable doesn't mean you have to share your life story. What it does mean is that you can admit your mistakes and fallibility: "That didn't go well." "I don't understand this. Help me out here." "I'm worried about xyz."

Behaviors that generate trust relationships in workplaces are:

- Empathy, genuine concern, care, and compassion
- Ensuring disclosures or vulnerabilities are not shared outside of the immediate relationship
- Reliably enacting your professional role
- Sharing a vulnerability
- Providing valuable information that hasn't been sought
- Listening and acknowledging what you hear
- Responding to questions with both detail and precision
- Doing what you say you will do and communicating simply when that isn't possible
- Acknowledging your mistakes when you make them

Trust may take time to build, but it can be destroyed remarkably quickly. Here are four trust killers:

- Gossip—(betrayal): Using private information about someone or acting without their best interests in mind
- Breaking agreements
- Not listening, or simply disregarding what someone has said
- Uninvited and persistent criticism

Having trusted relationships is a powerful source of influence in understanding what is really happening in your organization and how people think and feel about what is going on. Building these relationships, though, means exercising your own trust, sometimes through the trial and error of learning whom to trust and how much to disclose. It also means learning to repair relationships when trust is broken.

Trust is built when people know you have heard them and understood what they are saying. Trust and professionalism go hand in hand. Do your customers and stakeholders trust you to listen and respond to their feedback? Do they trust you not to break your promises?

Others will be profoundly affected by your own emotional reactions. Many leaders and their staff fear emotional openness and frankness in conversation. What are these fears? They fear:

- Not being listened to
- Not being taken seriously
- Hurting the other person
- Provoking anger, sadness, or shame
- Vindictive responses and social isolation

Trust in any leadership team can be rapidly generated by discovering shared experiences.

Shared Experiences Underpin Relationships

At the heart of every positive relationship are mutual connections based on shared experiences, understandings, and values. Recognition of shared connections enables us to "be known." This in turn helps us relax and bring our genuine selves forward. We discover mutual connections through our interactions. For example, having worked well on the same team might be one shared experience, being accountants may be a second, and enjoying problem solving may be a third. How often have you met a new colleague only to discover you have both survived a crisis, grapple with a similar life dilemma, have a love of music, or lived somewhere unusual as a child? Strong, positive work relationships are built with multiple connections resulting from joint accomplishments and significant shared experiences, understandings, and values.

As a sociometrist, I work to expand relationships among leaders by uncovering shared connections. There are three types of criteria for establishing connections, each of which is purpose dependent:

1. *Diagnostic criteria:* Display existing connections to provide the group with information that will assist their work. "How long have you been in your current role?" and "What attracted you to joining this group?" are examples of diagnostic criteria.

2. *Action criteria:* Produce here-and-now choices of group members to strengthen their current interpersonal connections. Examples of action criteria are:

   - "Who here would you choose to coach you on a current dilemma?"

   - "Who would you choose as a confidant to discuss a current concern?"

   - "Who would you want to hear from in finding a solution to this challenge?"

   I would then investigate further. "Let x know why you chose them." These perceptions are personal and private, and making them public knowledge is a delicate issue. Working this way relies on trusting relationships among group members and with the leader.

3. *Strategic criteria:* Develop relationships among group members to assist in future work.

Strategic criteria might include "Who in our team would you strengthen a working relationship with to move the business forward?" "With whom do you want to create an innovative approach?"

By choosing and being chosen on specific criteria, group members have a clear picture of their *companions*. Making choices in situ of whom to include or not often stimulates participants to create new patterns of relationships, which benefits the work of the group.

Actively creating opportunities for people to discover shared experiences assists leaders in building trust. In working with leadership teams, I might ask people to "introduce themselves" by saying where they were born, what their birth order was, what their parents did, and one family message that assists them as a leader now. Invariably the stories leaders tell reveal many connections with their peers. They deepen their appreciation of one another and how they might better work together.

Each new exploration gives the team information about itself that enables positive developments. One example in particular stands out.

CASE STUDY: JANICE AND HER TEAM

I was working with an energy sector leadership team. Janice, the team leader, told me that when she commissioned work, she felt exhausted by her team's predictable and continuous push-back. It was as if everyone was trying to be the boss. I believed that by expanding the connections among group members, they would develop greater appreciation of one another's contributions. This would most likely shift their focus from how work should be done to expanding their knowledge of what each person bought to the team's work. Early in our team session, I led an exercise to explore what these connections might be. As we stood in a circle, I asked such questions as, "In the past few months, who here has had a major success?" and "Who here is grappling with setting priorities?" With each criterion, I invited group members to step forward and share their experience. As team members responded positively, I decided to move to more personal territory. Intuitively, I asked, "Who here is the eldest in their family?" Everyone stepped forward! And as they did, they burst out laughing. I invited everyone to share one stereotype of being an eldest child that helps them as a leader and one saying that holds them back.

Team members drew together and began solving problems of work flow, priority setting, and collaboration.

Discovering shared experiences gives people a holistic appreciation of one another. But respectfully and purposefully working with the revelations of group members is essential. Uncovering shared connections within teams relies on

- The purpose of the group.
- The development outcomes being sought.
- The underlying development themes in the group.
- The nature of the current connections.
- The context of the group's work.

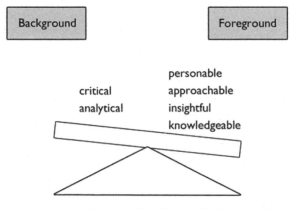

FIGURE 2.3 How Do You Want to Be Perceived?

The two identities, personal and professional, can be in conflict. Have you ever encountered the hostile accountant, the unhelpful IT manager, the abrasive marketer, or the obtuse strategic adviser? While they may have strong positive relationships with their bosses, they create anxiety and are feared by staff.

By establishing the relationship between your personal qualities and your professional identity, you can choose which of these you want to bring to the fore and which might be more effective in the background.

CASE STUDY: INGRID

Ingrid is CFO in a financial services company. An experienced accountant, she works well with senior leaders and provides solid advice and direction. She understands that C-suite leaders prefer complex things explained simply as she outlines the implications and financial risks of business decisions. However, within her team, Ingrid is rarely available, sets unworkable deadlines, and cuts off people when they speak.

I met with Ingrid and her manager, Adrian, to shape the coaching contract. Adrian reported her professional qualities were that she was knowledgeable, skilled, and experienced with organization finances. Adrian went on to say her staff perceived her as demanding, arrogant, unrealistic, and uncaring. They didn't trust her to be fair, to help them, or to back them up. Both Ingrid and Adrian were concerned that her personal qualities negatively affected her staff's experience of her.

Ingrid was capable of empathy. She understood the business drivers, the shifting contexts in which senior leaders operate, and what they required to make good decisions. Adrian commented her ability to size up situations rapidly, let her staff know the implications, and assist them in adjusting priorities would make a significant difference to her staff's experience both of her and their work. Ingrid's story unfolded. She was the only child of appreciative parents. Rapidly promoted thanks to her skills as accountant, the fact that staff needed to be managed never occurred to Ingrid. She assumed they would self-organize and was appalled and frustrated to realize they needed her help. "Why can't they just get on with it? It's obvious what needs to be done," she complained to me. Diana: "What a great question—let's find out." I suggested Ingrid make a sculpture using small figures to represent her, her team members, the work, the context, the C-suite leaders, and the business outcomes.

After her initial shock of seeing both the complexity of her work context and the fact that members of her team were not like her, Ingrid became curious. She and I discussed how she learned. Ingrid realized how much she had benefited from her parents' and bosses' good treatment and decided she would lead by appreciation.

Instead of snapping orders, she started using such phrases as "How can I help you?", "What do you need to complete this by Friday?", "I know that was a tough ask, and I love what you have produced. Your ability to nail the new indicators was helpful," and "This really fits the bill. Next time, go ahead and send me the first draft. I can help you shape it from there." By developing working relationships with her staff, Ingrid shifts from being a *demanding automaton* to a *personable results-oriented coach*. While her technical expertise is essential for her role, her personal qualities are essential for building her team and influence in the workplace.

Real Leaders Are Close to the People They Lead

We have used the word "leader" to distinguish a way of being, as if leading is more rarefied than managing. Where everyday managers focus on staff performance and creating business plans and reports, leaders have been more associated with influence and strategy. Theoretically, the distinction between leading and managing is this: Managing relates to maintaining the status quo and delivering results; leading relates to creating an organization's future and taking people with you.

It is a trap for a leader to believe they are separate from those they lead or are somehow elevated above them. Real leaders are an integral part of the people they lead and work actively to create open channels of communication with them. They know how and when to create emotional accessibility and distance between themselves and others.

People working with leaders with presence know that both they themselves and the work they are doing are important. Leaders who confuse social accessibility with emotional accessibility frequently struggle with setting priorities. The ten-minute meeting where both parties connect with conversations that matter beats the formulaic hour-long meeting every time.

First Impressions Count

In any moment when we meet a new colleague, our minds and all of our perceptive capacities work in overdrive as we make unconscious assessments and develop initial impressions. Are we drawn toward them or not? Are they approachable, friendly, or influential in relation to us? Are they standoffish, offhand, or likely to remain under the radar? Much of my work is concerned with making these initial impressions and assessments conscious. This helps leaders know the qualities they convey when they show up.

CASE STUDY: INITIAL IMPRESSIONS

Beginning an executive presence session with senior leaders from different agencies meeting for the first time. The group was underway. People had introduced themselves by identifying a moment they first realized they were a leader. Formal introductions come later. I work with two principles early in groups. This first is to have people meet one another using a criterion each person associates with. The second is to bring out initial impressions of one another. Initial impressions influence people whether they are drawn to or away from one another, yet these remain private and unspoken. In most situations this second approach would be unwise. While group members have just met, I have met with each one and know the outcomes they are seeking and something of their background. I also know the development themes in the group, and my criteria are based on this earlier research.

I invited Tim to choose among his peers: "Who here looks like a leader?" Of course Tim is immediately on the spot. Making assessments of people yet to introduce themselves to one another is risky. However, he trusts me and my intentions. He takes a deep breath and chooses: Andrea, Michael, Brad, Ellie. I then ask, "What is it about Andrea that makes you choose her?" "It was the way she stands with confidence and how her eyes rest gently on the group."

"Why did you choose Michael?" "He looks relaxed and easy in himself, and his eyes convey curiosity." "I chose Brad because he is casually and well dressed. His body is still. He looks calm. His shoulders are back, and his face looks 'open.'" Group members who have been chosen look pleased. Those who haven't been chosen are curious and thoughtful.

They are comparing what they are hearing with their own observations. We continue exploring first impressions on a number of criteria. Some people are highly chosen, others less so. Each leader learns how they might be perceived in the initial moments of group life. They can reflect on this and decide whether this is how they want to be perceived.

Astonishingly, leaders with presence have simple behaviors to ensure people feel *included*. They are relaxed and still, they look people gently in the eye, and they communicate simply. They smile and look interested in those around them, indicating *approachability*. They introduce themselves and let people know what they think and how they feel. These ostensibly small things have significant impacts in helping leaders develop relationships rapidly and make others feel included. Leaders who tend to fidget, avoid looking at people or move their eyes rapidly, stand awkwardly, or have poor posture are less likely to be chosen by their peers as "looking like a leader."

Social Intelligence

Social intelligence is the capacity to both navigate a range of drivers and function effectively within formal and informal networks. Leaders function in groups whether they like it or not, as their identity and *acceptance* as leader is completely reliant on the groups they are part of. On the surface, leaders are only differentiated by their purpose and role, but this is not the whole story. Others decide what kind of leader you are from their experience of working with you. With this in mind, leading fantastic group meetings is a core attribute for any leader. However, HBR Research found that

- Sixty-five percent of meetings were about "information sharing," "group input," or "group discussion," rather than making decisions.
- Only 12 percent of executives believed that their meetings

consistently produced decisions on important strategic or organizational issues.[1]

This is one major source of frustration with rational leaders: their
frequent inability to work well with people in meetings. They act as if *being
the leader* were their function rather than *leading people*. Separating *people*
from the professional *leader* is a mistake. "Social Intelligence is the ability
to get along well with others, and to get them to cooperate with you."[2] The
ability to maintain relationships and communicate effectively when under
pressure is key to executive presence yet remains a serious oversight with
most approaches to leadership development, as we will see in chapter 6.

The main artifact codifying leadership roles and structural hierarchy is the organization chart, which gives visibility to lines of reporting.
Structural relationships are based on two assumptions: (1) that everyone has clear roles and responsibilities and (2) that the relationships are
one-way—from leader to staff, leader to peers, and leader to bosses. But
organization charts fail to show other important informal organization
structures:

- How work gets done
- Who influences whom
- Who consults with whom
- Who discusses ideas with whom
- Who intimidates whom
- Who relies on whom for information about the organization
- Who trusts whose insights on the wider context

Informal organizational structures are networks made up of people
who get together because they *want* to, not because they have to. Leaders
with presence understand the nature of these informal network structures

---

[1] Mankins, "Stop Wasting Valuable Time," *Harvard Business Review.*
[2] Albrecht, *Social Intelligence.*

as well as the power of interpersonal connections. They recognize central players in the informal networks and develop relationships with them, either directly or through someone connected to them.

Leaders' capacity to function effectively in social settings is crucial. Looking at an organization chart can fool us—on a logical and rational level—into thinking we know how people work together and who works with whom. Roles and responsibilities are delineated, so what could possibly go wrong? What creates turmoil is the myriad of invisible relationships based on who wants to work with whom, and conversely, who doesn't want to work with whom. This is evidenced by gaps and overlaps in roles or boundaries. Why do gaps and overlaps mess things up?

Gaps and overlaps have disparate and distinctive origins. A gap is created when no one knows who has responsibility, or no one takes responsibility. A leadership gap results in relationship breakdown within the organization, and nothing gets done. This has an emotional impact on those affected. When a tough issue comes up, the buck is passed and no one steps up to say, "This is me; this is my role." When two or more organizations unused to working together join forces, do things always go smoothly? Of course not. Both organizations focus on the project that must be done, but gaps tend to appear. Each organization thinks the other will handle it, and neither organization takes responsibility.

CASE STUDY: CLOSING THE GAP

A corporate services group was feeling overwhelmed by customer feedback complaining about inefficiency and irrelevancy. Tough stuff indeed. The group recently reformed to be customer-centric and the GM decided to investigate. After consulting with customers, the GM and his team became aware that *all* policies for travel, leave, and refunds were recorded on the website. Every historic iteration was there. It was impossible for staff to know which one was current—a gap that created much frustration. Processing travel applications was cumbersome and time consuming. A gap between leaders of the business groups widened, with other GMs complaining.

The GM of corporate services decided to take responsibility and formed a team including customers together with staff from administration, policy, and communications, and reviewed the processes. They asked questions like "What frustrated you the most in . . . ." **Action:** All obsolete policies were deleted. The website was clarified, and accessing information was made simpler and accurate. The processing time for travel applications and refunds reduced and the relationship between the business groups and corporate services warmed.

Overlaps occur when two or more people or parties act as if they have the same responsibility. The two parties are trying to do the same thing. One says, "That's my job," and the other claims, "No, that's my job." Typical examples include boards interfering in operations, executive micromanagement, business units not communicating, and sales departments generating orders that production can't fill. Gaps and overlaps also appear when the lines between national and local government blur and in large-scale multidimensional emergencies.

Misunderstandings occur, people clash, tensions rise, and people suffer. Duplicated work doesn't make it twice as good; it is expensive at best and wasteful at worst.

When people don't know one another or are resistant to collaboration, such gaps and overlaps create havoc. A gap leads to inaction; an overlap creates duplicates work.

Problems of overlaps occur all the time in mergers and acquisitions. Both companies try to do the same thing, and people begin fighting one another. When people don't know which version to pay attention to, they become frustrated and panic.

Gaps, overlaps, and noncommunication within teams, companies, and boardrooms cause many business failures and service breakdowns. Leadership is either absent or confused. These are issues that leaders with presence tackle using both their personal and professional qualities. Focusing on the shared outcome, they identify sources of tension and create opportunities for people to hear one another's perspectives. They find ways forward.

Leaders who know how to help others have a strong basis for collaboration. They

- Share what is going on in the organization or wider context.
- Show them how to get things done.
- Serve as confidants or sounding boards to test ideas.
- Solve problems collaboratively.
- Share information.
- Manage risks.
- Give recognition.
- Listen to ideas and concerns.
- Appreciate them as people.

Relationships based on these actions enable work to be done. Successful leaders can navigate both formal structures and informal networks to get what they need done. They know the key informal influencers, both positive and not so positive. They know who others talk to and they know who has relationships across several groups. They either develop relationships with these people or are close to people who do. When leaders understand these networks, psychological safety in organizations is improved. People are confident in leaders who know what is going on or who are likely to take them seriously if they speak up.

Why Would Anyone Want to be Led by You?

What draws people to you? Why would they want to be led by you? What helps us, as leaders, to inspire others? What makes people move away from you?

Psychiatrist, prolific social researcher, and author Jacob Moreno, founder of the field of sociometry, identified two types of criteria for understanding what attracts people: sociotelic and psychetelic.[3] Sociotelic

---

[3] Moreno, *Who Shall Survive?*

criteria correspond to the social identity of the leader: intelligence and qualifications; job roles such as manager, doctor, leader, marketer, accountant; and skills such as analyst, writer, debater, listener, intellectual, or planner. The sociotelic identity of a leader on its own is soulless and lifeless.

What gives life to the leader's sociotelic identity are psychetelic criteria—their private, personal attributes and subjective identity.[4] Psychetelic criteria correspond to the dramatic element of the leader's social identity. Their psyche profoundly influences how they enact their function. Personal attributes that attract others include trust, inclusivity, curiosity, imagination, care, helpfulness, vision, wisdom, thoughtfulness, decisiveness, logic, and rationality. Personal attributes that repel others include anger, grandiosity, frustration, and aggression.

Leaders express their personalities through their behavior and actions, which influence the experience that others have of them. This implies that the personality is outside of the body rather than in some private, internal experience.[5] Leaders operating solely from their psychetelic identity typically won't fit in the work culture. They form relationships based on emotional predilections rather than on the work that needs to be done.

How leaders enact their roles relies on the relationship between their sociotelic (professional) and psychetelic (personal) identity. These two identities are differentiated, but by consciously blending them, leaders can effectively combine their professional skills and experience to enhance their social intelligence.

Somewhere along the line, the idea of being professional came to imply emotionless objectivity above all else. This belief devalued people and raised the task in hand above human considerations. An example of this is war. Winning territory and gaining political supremacy becomes more important to leaders than people's lives. People killed in war are referred to as "collateral damage." That "human resources" departments still exist in organizations beggars belief.

---

[4] Hale, *Conducting Clinical Sociometric Explorations*; Williams, *Forbidden Agendas*.
[5] Moreno, *Sociometry and the Cultural Order*.

Leaders who have a conscious relationship between their personal and professional identities are able to make use of their experience, intuition, and vision as well as their knowledge and expertise. It is impossible to wholly separate your emotions from your professional self; what is possible is to use your emotions wisely. It is for this reason that Daniel Goleman's work in emotional intelligence made sense to many leaders.

Some leaders make the mistake of indiscriminately discussing their personal experiences or feelings without first establishing a mutual connection on a specific work-related criterion. Leaders who do this create an emotional dependency; staff are expected to be productive while caring and even being responsible for their leader's emotional life. This is not workable.

CASE STUDY: SAM

Sam is stressed. A C-suite leader, she'd been stung by feedback from her CEO after she had dropped the ball on a major project. The CEO was furious. Sam fretted. She couldn't sleep and she lost the ability to see the bigger picture and make people decisions rapidly. She feared losing her job. After she confided in her staff what was happening, they began tiptoeing around her. They stopped bringing their concerns to her. They sensed she had lost interest in them, and they were right.

Leaders with presence share their insights and personal experience related to matters at hand and maintain positive relationships with others. Many leaders carry complex personal experiences privately. In the span of only two months, I worked with two leaders who had partners with terminal illnesses, several with teenagers with debilitating health conditions, and others facing unexpected bereavements. These are the everyday experiences of successful leaders. Few would know what was going on other than close friends, trusted bosses, or colleagues. These personal experiences remain private, but they deeply affect each leader. The qualities these leaders bring to the fore are understanding, compassion, and thoughtfulness. These are the psychetelic criteria people around them respond to.

Leaders and Their Relationships Create Culture

Leaders can shape culture by adjusting their interactions with one another and their interactions with their staff. The U.K.-based Hay Group found that

> Up to 70 percent of a team's climate is determined by the leader and leaders creating high performing climates have a broader range of styles in which authoritative, affiliative, democratic and coaching are dominant. Less successful leaders have fewer styles and rely mainly on coercion and pacesetting.[6]

Leaders reluctant to take responsibility for shaping company culture overlook an essential part of their function. If there is bullying in the organization, you are likely to find aggressive behavior around the leadership table. Where there are surprise resignations of key personnel, you can be sure that there is a lack of honesty or trust in the boardroom, resulting in poor communication of what is important.

Where interpersonal and intergroup tensions create problems within an organization, people have emotional responses. Anyone who has led a major change—be it a restructuring or a financial cutback—knows staff become anxious in response to events outside their control. The emotional culture of any group affects their capacity to produce results.

> Positive emotions are consistently associated with better performance, quality and customer service. . . . On the flip side, negative emotions such as group anger, sadness and fear and the like usually lead to negative outcomes, including poor performance and high turnover.[7]

As with any system, leaders will find that their overdeveloped default behaviors are reflected in other parts of the organization. On the positive side, when leaders attend to their behavior, creating productive cultures becomes easier.

---

[6] Hay Group, "Insight to Impact: Leadership That Gets Results."
[7] Barsade and O'Neill, "Manage Your Emotional Culture," *Harvard Business Review.*

Whom Do You Choose?

Leaders flourish when they have a personal network of trusted companions based on specific criteria. Possessing a network of people meeting the nine criteria below will ensure you remain on the front foot. With each new position you are appointed to, redeveloping relationships based on these criteria is essential. Ideally, everyone in your organization has people around them they choose to work with. The nine criteria are:

- Who inspires me to do my job?
- Whom can I solve problems with?
- Whom do I go to to find out what is going on in the organization?
- Who has creative ideas that work?
- Who knows how the system really works?
- Whom can I confide in?
- Who confides in me?
- Who has their eye out for me and my future?
- Who would let me know if I am being inappropriate in any way?

Who chooses you on these criteria? Your psychological equilibrium is determined by knowing who is important to you and vice versa. The smallest number of people needed to maintain your equilibrium is known as your *psychological social atom*. If a key member of your current social atom leaves, or if you move to a new organization, unless you rapidly regenerate new trusted relationships on these criteria, you can become distracted and defensive. Feelings of loss of significant others can divert your creative productive orientation as you struggle to maintain or replace that connection.[8] Some leaders have many people they relate to on each criterion; others have only one person associated with each criterion.

---

[8] Hale, *Conducting Clinical Sociometric Explorations*, 21.

The Leader as Detective

Leaders must often act as if they were detectives. They have two tasks. The first is to become alert to their own default behaviors. This means developing self-awareness and finding trusted confidants to let them know when they are inappropriate. The second is more complex. It's about:

- Being aware of the positive and negative impacts made by staff and peers.
- Accepting the responsibility to assist people to make positive contributions.
- Having courage and trusting relationships with those people.
- Perceiving and simply describing different behaviors and their impact.

Gathering information, making discoveries, informally testing perceptions, and making conclusions are the leader's responsibility. When these tasks go undone,

- Projects fail.
- People step over lines they didn't know existed.
- Organizations are needlessly restructured.
- Performance reviews are time wasting and meaningless.
- Political interventions take precedence over customer relations.
- Accountability is lost.

Leaders' self-awareness of their positive impacts enables them to replicate these behaviors and produce results. People will be drawn to them. Knowing their negative impacts helps them to take stock and adjust. If they choose not to listen to those around them, they lose their positive relationships as people remain neutral or move away from them. I do not mean "moving away" in the physical sense; it is an emotional withdrawal.

Emotionally driven behaviors that cause others to become fearful or withdraw are

- Anger and frustration, shouting, blaming, and accusations.
- Criticizing and judging others; belittling comments.
- Leaders relying solely on logic or their intellect to communicate in response to their own or others' unexpressed fears.

Leaders' relationship between their personal and professional identities directly affects their capacities for inspiring relationships.

Practice Session 2.1: Your Psychological Social Atom

Who are your trusted confidants? Identify two or three people meeting each criterion.

- Who among your boss, peers, and staff would be aware if you were stressed or upset?
- Whom can you confide in about almost anything?
- Who would drop what they were doing to listen to you when you needed help?
- For whom would you drop what you were doing?
- Who helps you see the funny side of things?
- Whom do you confide in?
- It would be hard for me to be motivated in my work without . . .

What insights do you have as you reflect on your choices of trusted confidants?

Practice Session 2.2

List four positive qualities you have and two qualities that hinder your effectiveness.

1. Write each one on a sticky note.

2. Bring to mind a situation where you responded less effectively than you wanted to.

3. Place the sticky notes according to which qualities are currently in the foreground and which are in the background.

4. Move these so the qualities helpful for your current situation are in the foreground, and place the less helpful qualities in the background.

What would it take for you to make this shift?

Summary

- Without personal qualities, leaders are faceless bureaucrats.
- Our experience of being with any leader is greatly influenced by their personal qualities.
- Your professional identity is shaped by choosing what is personal, what is private, and what you let come to the foreground in your interactions.
- Real leaders are close to the people they lead.
- Small things significantly impact leaders' ability to develop relationships rapidly and make others feel included.
- Your own emotional reactions influence what others experience.
- Maintaining relationships and communicating effectively with others under pressure is your key to executive presence.
- Establish the relationship between your personal and professional self using your experience, intuition, and vision as well as your knowledge, expertise, and relationships.
- Being aware of who is in your network of trusted relationships and knowing who chooses you, creates your sense of psychological security.

Chapter 3

How Relationships Work

WE'VE SEEN THAT MAINTAINING RELATIONSHIPS and emotional equilibrium under stressful conditions is more important than technical acumen. These capacities are prerequisite for inspiring others, as leaders with presence remain steady under pressure. This chapter shows how you can do so.

Staying calm under stress is as difficult for leaders as it is for anyone else. Leaders with presence might well react emotionally to a given challenge—they are human, after all. Leaders with presence both feel strongly *and* are able to activate their thinking. If their emotional response is too overwhelming, they stand still, give themselves room, and take small steps until they are able to think with a clear head. The key thing here is that leaders with presence stay in relationship with those around them even in extreme circumstances.

When leaders flip out and act overemotionally, they disturb people. Those around them become anxious and fearful. It's as if the leader has put up a wall between them and people around them. The organization becomes unsettled. When the leader is steering the ship, you want to know whether they can keep it together. How can leaders remain even-keeled?

Of course, feeling upset, frustrated, disappointed, or stressed is normal. More problematic is if you are frequently upset and stressed and when you act from your emotions without thinking.

Discovering your genuine self— what you think and feel on important matters—is essential for any leader. Equally important is knowing

- Your values.
- Where these values come from.
- How they relate to your current context.
- Why you do what you do.
- The quality of relationships you want to have with people.

Ask yourself: Are my values still workable for me in the current context?

Organizations are influenced by a myriad of political, social, and economic factors. The complexities created by people and relationships give leaders time-consuming and gut-wrenching problems. Key staff unexpectedly leave, a major deadline is missed, fraud is revealed, executives can't stand one another, key stakeholders reject your product or service, a merger fails, your relationship with the board chair deteriorates—these are all everyday events. You are likely to respond emotionally to each of these.

Leaders' presence is determined by whether they act from their initial emotional responses or whether they align their thinking with their emotions *while* maintaining relationships. Understanding shifts in relationships—and their positive or negative emotional impacts—helps leaders to navigate complex terrain. Their emotional responses are influenced by shifts in relationships in their own lives: a close friend moves away, a significant relationship ends, or they fight with someone dear to them. Similarly, movements in business relationships have an emotional effect; an adversarial colleague joins your team, a loved boss unexpectedly leaves, or valued colleagues are laid off.

Leaders with executive presence know how relationships work. They know "right relationships" and that when someone is destructive in their group, they need to act. They can recognize when a group is working well together and when it is working poorly. They know when to intervene or let events take their natural course.

Some believe that executive presence is only about the leader maintaining a professional appearance and being a good communicator. But leaders with real presence must be able to *read* relationships. Executive presence is not all about you, leader; it's how you deal with board members, colleagues, employees, customers, stakeholders, and members of the public *and* get things done. How do *you* respond effectively in times of conflict? How do *you* navigate those situations?

Leaders with presence stay active in their relationships. In times of stress, they keep open lines of communication with staff, peers, stakeholders—and themselves. They can't just dress well and speak well to have presence; they do all that *and* work well with people.

Doubt and Confidence

Many leaders I work with doubt themselves and lose confidence when they sense they could "do better." Leaders flourish when they have a positive relationship with their personal self, knowing their inner lives are a rich source of leadership material. They accept themselves their strengths and their weaknesses. They accept they are not perfect, and they expect to learn. By exploring earlier experiences, leaders can identify influences on their behaviors, values, and beliefs and assess what could be relevant to their current context. By doing so, they (1) become conscious of why they are chosen for leadership roles and (2) find leading others easier.

Making Sense of Relationships

Sociometry can help leaders make sense of working relationships. The basic premise of sociometry is that there are at least three entities in each relationship: the individuals and the relationships between them. The relationship connects the first two entities.

Relationships can sometimes be thought of as being invisible, but we can make relationships explicit using simple diagrams (see below). We can then see and respond to what we are sensing and feeling and—more importantly—choose the qualities we want to have in our relationships.

FIGURE 3.1   Qualities in a Positive Interpersonal Relationship

FIGURE 3.2   Qualities in a Negative Interpersonal Relationship

At least four main relationship categories exist. They are:

1. Intrapsychic: the relationship between personal and professional identities within a person
2. Interpersonal: the relationship between two people
3. One to many: the relationship of a person with a group and vice versa
4. Intergroup: relationships between groups

Leaders improving relationships in any one of these categories enhances their capacities in the others. The overall quality of the intrapsychic relationship between personal and professional identities shapes leaders' behaviors in all other relationships and events.

On the one hand, leaders who

- Second-guess themselves
- Don't push back when their ideas are challenged
- Avoid conflict
- Excessively express their annoyance, frustration, and anger
- Change their minds frequently

- Are silent on important matters
- Are overly critical of themselves and others

have a negative intrapsychic relationship with themselves. Those around them become confused and emotionally draw away. On the other hand, leaders who

- Actively listen
- Back themselves
- Have the difficult conversations so people know where they stand
- Show how they think and feel in their actions
- Accept conflict as a core part of life and engage wisely
- Describe the real picture
- Continue to share vision and direction under pressure

have positive intrapsychic relationships. People are drawn to them.

The quality of interpersonal relationships among people, and between leaders and their staff, creates an organization's culture.[1] Organizational culture can be described as "how we do things around here." By changing their behavior, individuals and groups can shift the quality of their relationships and change group culture. Being conscious of the culture leaders want to create will influence their interactions with individuals and groups.

CASE STUDY: SHIFTING THE EMOTIONAL TONE

Advising a prison leadership team in a strategy session, I was taken aback. The leaders were rude and cynical with one another. I knew jokes and war stories were part of their culture, but this was something else. I sensed the emotional tone in this group was an entangled ball of hurt

---

[1] Jones, Diana "The Way We Do Things around Here."

and angry feelings. Disturbed, I asked, "What is behind you talking with one other like this?" The team knew what I was referring to. "We talk to each other like this all the time. In an emergency we have to be straight with one another. None of us take it personally." I agreed, "Yes, in an emergency; however, this is day-to-day business. What would be gained if you related to one another respectfully?" Someone cracked a joke about being touchy-feely. "I'm not asking you to touch one another. I am proposing that you to talk with one another as if you like working together. Let's move on. What other means do you have to reduce drugs getting to inmates?" The content of the discussions shifted from accusations to strategies. The emotional tone of the interactions shifted from one of irritating one another to laughing and enjoying the possibilities they were generating.

People's responses to one another create the "emotional tone" in a group. While nothing may be said, the interpersonal feelings projected among people have a significant impact on the emotional tone in any group. Where the flow of feeling among group members is positive, people share their ideas and perspectives and make decisions, resulting in productive meetings. Where the flow of feeling is fraught, people become guarded, fearful, or aggressive.

Empathy

Empathy is our capacity to sense and relate to others feelings, emotions, attitudes, and desires. Empathy is one-way—one-way in that there is no expectation that the other might reciprocate. You, as leader, are "there" for the other.

Leaders who stand in the shoes of others are "in" the relationship. They know relationships are two-way. People feel heard and understood by them. You, as a leader, are "with" them. Leaders who refuse or are unable to relate to those around them are regarded as cold and heartless.

How Do You Demonstrate Empathy?

Leaders have several options when relating to others; however, the keys to success is to maintain their leadership role, be clear about the purpose and desired outcome of their interactions and be empathetic.

By recognizing and mirroring the "feeling" state of those they are with, leaders give people confidence that they understand their position.

"What I am about to say is likely to be the last thing you want to hear. We are closing this part of the business. I want each and every one of you to know . . . "

"What we have been doing has been hard work. We have entered a new phase . . .

Leaders lose their power to influence if they can't show they understand the people they lead. Leaders' empathy is at the heart of capturing hearts and minds.

The Tele Connection

Something beyond the traditional concept of empathy is required to account for the complex dynamics of work relationships. Relationships are not one-way, they are two-way between people, and multidimensional among people. Where "empathy" falls short in organizations is that its one-way nature leaves staff and peers unaccountable for their part in the relationship.

The field of sociometry gives us language and concepts to help us describe what is occurring. Jacob Moreno influenced many people in the field of interpersonal and group relations with his concept of "tele," the two-way flow of feeling between people. Tele connotes distance; for example, "telecommunications" means communication at a distance. Tele reflects the socioemotional distance between people based on measures of companionship. Understanding tele adds to any psychological and socio-logical assessment of choices of people as they move toward and away from one another. The flow of feeling is two-way, both projected and retrojected—like a two-ended stick. Both entities are "in" the relationship.

Have you ever walked into a room and sensed tension? "You could cut the air with a knife" is an expression used when there is an evident atmo-sphere of negative feeling. Conversely, the expression "There is energy in the room" reflects the positive flows of feeling among the people there. Tele is the basis of interpersonal chemistry, the feeling of attraction or repulsion that relates to our interpersonal responses to people.

Within any group, people are "attracted" to one another or with-draw in a manner analogous to magnetic attractions and repulsions. As you meet people in your work, you are immediately drawn to some and instinctively avoid others. Positive tele enables you to understand a person and have insight into their qualities before you have gotten to know them. You have experienced positive tele if you have ever quickly "hit it off" with someone without knowing them well. Invariably, your initial assessment is accurate. Negative tele results in personality clashes or negative vibes.

The intensity of tele—which likely emanates in the brain's limbic sys-tem—can be subjectively measured as weak or strong and either positive, negative, or neutral. Tele is a form of two-way empathy: from you to the other person and vice versa.

With positive tele, we feel like we really "get" another person or group and have instant rapport. We move "closer."

With negative tele we want to "move away" or avoid the person. This is a crucial point. Negative feelings of discomfort and "not understand-ing" another's values can lead to unhelpful assumptions and stereotyping. This in turn can result in being critical or mocking when interpreting the other person's or group's behavior. These responses are entirely unhelpful and lead to mutually rejecting relationships. The distance between people widens and emotional responses tend to drive action.

Basing work relationships on the criterion of "liking" is irrelevant. If you must work with someone you would rather not, sometimes collaboration is possible. Frequently, you learn that a "difficult" person has invaluable qualities:

- They simplify complex ideas in a way that helps communicate the big picture.
- Their political know-how helps to find solutions.
- Their fearlessness in conflict enables you both to draw the best out and influence key stakeholders.
- Their capacity for detail provides a pragmatic approach for implementing strategy.

Working relationships based on work criteria assist people who on first response want to reject one another. By differentiating their negative response it is possible to move from "not liking" to finding productive ways to work together. The negative response would most likely mean you would not have a friendship or undertake social activities together.

With neutral tele, we have no initial "sense" of the other. Only by working together and having shared experiences are tele relationship bonds strengthened.

Executive presence requires leaders to develop strategies for creating positive flows of feeling. When you are with someone with presence, you are receptive to their influence regardless of whether you know them well. There is an attraction there. In a group, the same experience applies. Mutual positive connections inspire people to take action, leading to progress and forward movement.

This is where the rubber hits the road. Positive mutual tele among group members generates social cohesion, where negative tele destroys social cohesion.

The capacity to generate positive connections with peers and staff resides with leaders. The work cultures they create, the meetings they produce, the conversations they have, and the directions they give provide opportunities to create greater cohesion.

Those with executive presence actively generate
positive flows of feeling among those around them.

Reading the "flow" of feeling accurately requires you to develop interpersonal perception, the ability to *read people* and *read a room*. By *reversing roles* and actively seeing the situation through others' eyes, you can dramatically increase your ability to read people's behavior and tailor your communication.

PRACTICE SESSION

Imagine yourself walking toward your senior leadership team. What is your sense of the flow of feeling from you to them, and from the team to you? Do you sense a negative flow of feeling—as if the group is "out to get you"? If you have no strong sense of the purpose of your participation, or low awareness of your interpersonal capacities, you are likely to be anxious or nervous. In doing so, you generate a negative flow of feeling toward the group, and those in the group can sense this. The stakes are high in these interactions: You want to do a good job, while the group wants to know how you can help them. What might you do to generate a mutual positive flow of feeling?

    You might

1. Decide how you can help this group.
2. Bring to mind both your purpose and theirs.
3. Vividly imagine the ideal outcome of your meeting with the group.

In chapter 2, we learned tele relationships can be generated in groups by using specific criteria to enable people to make choices.

A diagram such as figure 3.3 is helpful for showing the closeness or distance between people in a moment in time. The density of lines shows the degree of importance to the business, while plus and minus signs signify the degree of trust in each relationship. You can create a diagram of your current team relationships and see how well they suit the team's purpose and current context. A similar diagram can be constructed to reflect progress in purposeful relationships. Figure 3.3 indicates this leader has work to do in turning around his or her relationships with at least three direct reports, Barry, Ellen, and Brigit, and to ensure Brigit and Dean work well together in order to drive the business.

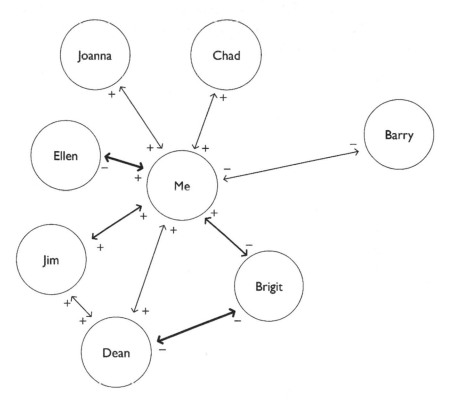

FIGURE 3.3 Sample Team Relationships: How Well We Work Together

What is it about you that generates positive flows of feeling from others? What qualities draw people to you or lead them to prefer others? What qualities do you have that might generate negative flows of feeling toward you? Knowing this enables you to expand your values and adjust your behavior.

To succeed as a leader, building positive mutual relationships is crucial. Of course there will always be people in your life that you want to avoid. Because you won't always have good working relationships, you must actively choose who you do want to work with. Use your intuition and judgment to build an informal network of trusted and trusting colleagues.

Executive appointments reveal an area where assessments of potential positive mutual tele is crucial. Solely relying on psychometrics for choosing executives is a flawed strategy because psychometrics considers neither interpersonal chemistry nor the context the candidate will be working in. Assessing a candidate's capacity to have positive relationships *and* get the job done is best done by personal intuition, wise judgment and reference checks.

CASE STUDY: BILL AND CHAD

Bill was delighted to appoint Chad as his operations manager. He came with excellent credentials and experience; just what Bill needed. Bill did have a reservation, though, shared by the chair of his board. They were both aware Chad had strong opinions and expressed them freely. Would he take direction? Backed by the chair of the board, Bill took the risk.

Over the next two months, Chad was intensely critical of what was going on in the organization. He was angry and frustrated that systems weren't in place. Chad expressed his disappointment to everyone with fault finding, criticism, and complaints. He rapidly alienated people. Chad acted as if he thought his ideas and observations were better than everyone else's.

Bill was divided. He desperately wanted Chad's skills. He could see positive actions being taken within the operational divisions. He could see some staff were warming to Chad with the new direction. He wanted his decision to appoint to work, but Chad was creating havoc in his leadership team. Meetings were a nightmare. Executives became guarded and unwilling to contribute to discussions. Several complained and one refused to meet with Chad. Bill's time was flooded with trying to understand what was happening, sorting out conflicts, and coaching Chad. Chad proved resistant. Bill could see factions developing. The negative tele Chad generated created a mutual response from his peers both individually and as a group. Valuing his own positive relationships with his leaders and them with one another, Bill came to the painful decision to let Chad go.

You are not going to have positive relationships with everyone around you. However, as a leader, your capacity to engage and unite people who have different views by communicating your vision and direction is essential. It is easy to be divisive. Excluding people on social criteria—such as country of origin, ethnicity, and religion—has especially dramatic and negative consequences, as we are currently seeing in deadly conflicts on the world stage.

Leaders who focus on one preferred population while excluding others create alienation and anger, as in Syria, Turkey, and much of the U.S. Creating unity is challenging for any leader. Successful leaders draw upon shared human experiences and inclusive visions to create social cohesion while remaining respectful of personal differences.

Mutual flows of positive feeling from leaders to others create an open two-way relationship for communication, acceptance, and understanding, and together, possibilities for the future can be created.

CASE STUDY: PETER

Peter was a seasoned VP. He had a reputation for delivering results, good interpersonal relationships, and being innovative. However, he found leading groups nerve-wracking. Each time he approached a group, he felt he was going to have to stand up and account for himself.

Obviously in leading organization-wide change projects, Peter experienced challenges from the groups he led. He would fret prior to leading a change session. His way of coping was to be blunt, perceptive, and direct in groups. Peter would enter a group ready for combat.

I asked Peter how he felt toward the group, and what his sense was of the flow of feeling from the group to him. As he reflected, he realized he felt negatively toward the group, generated by his anxieties and what he imagined. He sensed a negative flow from the group to him. I asked,

"What could be produced if your relationship with this group was posi-tive?" Peter was thoughtful.

I knew Peter well. I knew he was well liked and respected. It seemed his approach might be more habitual than current. I asked, "Have you thought of approaching groups as if they were your friends and compan-ions, not your competitors? Currently I notice you respond to others as if they were your enemies. Act on the assumption that group members are positive toward you and that they want to hear from you."

Peter learned to shift focus from his own anxieties and fears (of making mistakes, of not doing a great job, or of appearing ignorant) to the people he was with, their interests and concerns, and to their shared purpose.

Peter tried this new approach and later shared his observations with me. He noticed that people felt more included and participated more. He also noticed more readiness to listen and to engage with one another.

Peter learned that people wanted to hear what he had to say, even if it wasn't good news. By shifting his approach to entering groups, Peter's emotional expansiveness increased. He discovered he could be friendly and look forward to being in groups even where tough decisions had to be made and where different views existed.

He learned that when he reversed roles and saw the situation through their eyes, people connected with him as the leader.

In short, if you are open to others and accept their quirks, foibles, dreams, and ambitions, then you are likely to generate a positive flow of feeling toward them. If you are resentful, anxious, critical, hurt, or angry, you are likely to communicate a negative or ambivalent flow of feeling.

What helps leaders generate a positive flow of feeling toward groups is to learn precisely who is in the group and the range of drivers and concerns they have, and to relate this to your shared purpose. Find out the level of mutuality within the group: Who are in factions? What concerns do they form around? Then write down how *you* can help this group. By doing this, you are more likely to approach groups with a positive emotional flow of feeling. As you begin, tune into the flow of feeling among group members. Use this assessment to guide how you proceed. With groups where you sense anxiety or negativity, actively work to create unity among those there prior to moving on to business. One way you can do this is by asking inclusive questions. (See page 177.)

Reading and Responding to Invisible Forces

In addition to reading relationships, leaders are required to read and navigate a range of invisible forces. They appreciate context if they are to create a pathway forward. They move toward some and away from others. Without these capacities, simplistic extremes emerge: Brexit or Remain, "us and them," "You are with us or against us." These "bipolar" options are political tactics rather than components of leadership. They create divisions in businesses and society and overlook the multiplicity of nuanced responses, dumbing down what we know, think, and imagine. Exploring views along any two-dimensional continuum enables complex conversations to be grounded in reality. People share their views, their insights and their knowledge. Everyone sees where they stand and knows who influences one another. Creating relevant processes enabling mutual sharing of ideas and testing out different options remains a challenge for many leaders (see more on pages 118–119).

political

stakeholders

customers

social

governance

environmental

bosses

economic

employees

colleagues

cultural

the public

FIGURE 3.4   Leaders Read Invisible Drivers Affecting Their Work

Most leaders relate to invisible yet powerful drivers created by governance, social unity, customers, the public, the economy, peers, and staff. Tele, interpersonal perception, and empathy are valuable capacities for navigating this complex web of drivers and providing context, while the leader's and group's combined vision provides direction.

How do leaders find a way forward? Successful leaders use metaphors to gain the perspective needed to "rise above" their current situation and look out into the future:

- Take a helicopter view.
- Move from the dance floor to the balcony.
- Reverse roles; see the situation through others' eyes.
- Get out of the weeds and up onto the hills.

Closeness and Distance with Different Leadership Approaches

Measuring the distance between leaders and those they lead reveals the value of different leadership approaches. Leaders who are unavailable or disinterested in their staff's progress distance themselves from those around them. They isolate themselves from the very people they are leading. They ignore their responsibilities to their staff. They act as if they are negative to their staff or as if their staff are not important. In response, the staff don't engage and mutual negative tele is evident.

Autocratic leaders both create a distance and "elevate" themselves from those they lead. They believe they know best and that their way is the only way, which makes people feel overlooked, undervalued, or misunderstood. Resentments brew between these leaders and their followers. Negative mutual tele is enacted. Neither "chooses" the other, creating conditions for domination or mutiny.

Other leaders overempathize with those around them. They lose their way as they seek to be liked rather than respected. They prefer to consult rather than lead. They become closer to the people they lead than to the organization. This results in people feeling understood; however, they lose the benefit of the leader's wisdom, thinking, or experience. These leaders become more aligned to individuals, their immediate team, or customers, jeopardizing organization results.

Emotional Expansiveness

Why do some leaders relate easily to large numbers of people and others not? Your capacity for mutually positive relationships with a wide range of people is called your *emotional expansiveness*. People feel "close" to these leaders and vice versa. This is different from your *social expansiveness*, your actual number of work or social connections.[2]

Your emotional expansiveness might be limited if you experience strong feelings of anxiety prior to being with large groups or with people you don't already know.

Leaders with limited emotional expansiveness are more likely to

- Be flushed, perspiring, anxious, fidgety, or unable to concentrate.
- Overprepare, overmemorize, or become overly administrative.
- "Wing it," then fret.
- Experience increased heart rate or speak quickly.
- Excessively refer to their notes.

The audience regards this type of leader as nervous, removed, wooden, detached, or theoretical. Rather than focusing on how they can help the audience, these leaders tend to be overly attuned to their own feeling state, or how they think people perceive them.

Leaders with emotional expansiveness

- Are aware of their vision and the ultimate desired outcome.
- Understand what their audience wants and expects.

---

[2] Moreno, *Who Shall Survive? Foundations of Sociometry, Group Psychotherapy and Sociodrama.*

- Communicate with heart, clearly and pragmatically
- Make gentle eye contact with those present.
- Are not wedded to low-level details.

Leaders with these abilities make audiences feel they are included and understood, and group members are more likely to apply what they have learned.

The Past Influences the Present: Memory and Behavior

What might get in the way of establishing positive mutual relationships? In our everyday lives, there are several psychological processes operating in the background that affect capacity for relationships. Good leaders build relationships by using metaphors and stories to convey their perceptions in a relatable way.

Sigmund Freud used the term *transference* to describe how original events are transferred to current times. Freud used the relationship between a client and their therapist as his context. I propose that the concept of transference is equally applicable to our relationships in organizations—in fact, anywhere there are structural relationships, where one party has perceived authority over another.

Transference is the redirection of emotions that were originally felt in childhood onto a current situation or person. It may be that your colleague reminds you of your brother who continually put you down, or your boss might remind you of your critical father. When your boss is angry and shouting, you shrivel up inside rather than standing tall and responding, "Hold it right there." Or "What's the outcome you are hoping for right now?" There's an interference between the then and the here. Your feelings from past events are transferred over and interfere with the current situation. Similarly, your boss could well be feeling the frustration and anger they felt as their younger sister or brother kept messing up their carefully constructed sand castle or game app.

The ego, which cannot distinguish between past and present, assumes then is now and responds as if you were in the same situation. Your behavior is driven by your emotional response and is not informed by your thinking or the awareness of the here-and-now context. Transference is an indication of emotions tied to an earlier event which has not been adequately integrated. Empathy and tele responses indicate completed integration.

There are several alerts to transference being present in default behaviors. Three main clues to look for if you think that transference might be coloring your default behaviors: (1) reacting rather than responding, (2) inflexible behavior, and (3) situational inertia.

Familial Relationship Networks Meet Organization Structures

Organizations are social systems with clearly defined roles and responsibilities. Leaders' and staff roles are defined structurally in the organization chart and indicate the formal network of working relationships. In addition there are informal leaders—people others listen to and confide in and whose influence they accept on how things are done. These informal networks of relationships are influential in what gets done. Everyone of us has our own networks of both personal and professional relationships. These determine both our capacity for resilience and our abilities to be responsive. (Refer back to practice session 2.1)

There is another network of relationships, one that is personal and deeply influential. Known as your *original social and cultural atom*, this is the network of interrelationships and behavioral patterns derived from your original family dynamics and early life.[3] This holds the keys for unlocking glitches in your current interactions and is your prime source of leadership material.

The process for leaders' development is to:

- Be aware of their default response.
- Discover its impact on people and tasks.
- Identify which aspects of their response belong in the past.
- Decide whether to explore the original event, cut the ties between then and now, or go forward and generate options. Each approach works.

---

[3] Moreno, *Who Shall Survive?* 24, 42.

- Generate new options for fresh responses, options that enable leaders to maintain relationships under what were previously challenging or stressful situations.
- Identify indicators that the new approaches have the desired effect.
- Track progress.

Practice Session 3.1

Choose a leadership team you either lead or are a member of. Write down the group's purpose.

_____

What outcomes do you want from participating in this group?

_____

What three skills, qualities, and attributes do you have that help this group be effective? What three actions might you take to increase your emotional expansiveness?

Practice Session 3.2

Picture both your current state and your desired future state as you anticipate leading a large group. How might you lead this group?

_____

_____

Practice Session 3.3

Choose five significant people or groups.

1. Identify the impact of your current behavior on each one. Choose terms from below. Then identify the impact of their behavior on you. Which of the terms below apply to each relationship?
   - _Adversarial, critical, judgmental, competitive, blaming, disappointing_

- *Aggressive, demanding, punitive, dismissive, defensive*
- *Hesitant, passive, anxious, nervous, hidden, invisible, awkward, apologetic*
- *Collaborative, collegial, solution focused, inspiring, visionary*
- *Easygoing, influential, accountable, resourceful, innovative*
- *Funny, helpful, caring, friendly, insightful, human, empathetic, calming*

2. Describe the quality of relationship you want to have from here on.
3. What is one behavioral change you might make to shift this relationship?

Practice Session 3.4

Bring to mind someone who provokes a strong negative response in you. Whom do they remind you of? What was the relationship then? Make two columns, with the name of the original person on the left and the current person on the right. List the similarities between the two. Looking at the list, what are your insights?

Summary

- Maintaining emotional equilibrium under stressful conditions is a prerequisite for executive presence.
- The quality of relationships among leaders and between leaders and their teams is what creates an organization's culture.
- Responding to everyday events with your thinking and feelings aligned helps you maintain relationships and determines your presence.
- Leaders with executive presence know how relationships work.
- Effective leaders actively generate positive flows of feeling to those around them.
- Reading the feeling flow accurately helps leaders develop interpersonal perception, the ability to "read a room" and "read people."

- By reversing roles and actively seeing the situation through another's eyes, you dramatically increase your ability to read behavior.
- Your original social and cultural atom holds keys to glitches in your current behavior and interactions—this is your leadership material.

Chapter 4

Perception Is Everything

IN CHAPTER 3, we saw how invisible forces deeply affect leaders' success. This chapter looks at the role of another invisible force, perception. Your self-perceptions, together with the perceptions of others are essential for both your psychological health and getting an accurate picture of yourself. Once you have an accurate picture, you are free to decide what you want to do, if anything.

Knowing how others see you is valuable. How much weight you give to their perceptions will depend on (1) how important these people are to you and (2) how you want to be perceived. This chapter explores the nature of perceptions and how to develop and apply your own perceptive capacities.

Would you want to see yourself as others see you? Whom are you interested in hearing from? How would you act on the information you receive?

Leaders are frequently frustrated because other people's perceptions of their situation and their own reality often don't match. However, if you really want to help people, perception matters just as much as reality. How you are perceived as a leader is crucial for developing productive working relationships.

Many leaders who want greater executive presence fear letting others see their default behaviors. Certain behaviors become obvious over time: inflexibilities, repetitive behaviors that don't work, stress, frustrations, and awkwardness. When leaders discover how others perceive them, they usually have three responses. First, embarrassment. Someone might have spotted something they would prefer to remain under the carpet. Second, relief. Most people are relieved once something hidden is put out in the open. Relief also comes from having their inner experience *mirrored* back to them. Third, a sense of challenge; how might they either shift their inner experience or others' perceptions? Most leaders who establish a good connection between their own and others' perceptions no longer fear coming across as a fraud.

Knowing How You Are Perceived

One way to explore how perceptions form is to consider that we have several layers of experience at the same time. One layer is created by your own inner experience and the second layer is an outer layer created by your interactions with others. Leaders with dissonance between the inner and outer layers tend to act along a continuum of bravado and self-doubt. Leaders with presence ensure a close match between their two layers of experience. They know how they want to be perceived, actively reflect on their inner experience, and attend to others' perceptions of them.

The domain of perceptions is excellent territory for learning and insight. Perceptions form through our senses and attempts to make our experience coherent. So while we receive knowledge and information from the outside world, our purpose is to make sense of it.

Definition: Perceive: to become aware, understand.

1. To become aware of (something) directly through any of the senses, especially sight and hearing

2. To cause or allow the mind to become aware of (a stimulus): The ear perceives sounds.

3. To achieve understanding of; apprehend.[1]

---

[1] *The Free Dictionary*, "Perceive," www.thefreedictionary.com/perceive, 2016.

CASE STUDY: SØREN

Søren, an executive at a service delivery company, wanted to be known as a good people leader. He had excellent relationships with his board, clients, and stakeholders, yet his relationships with his direct reports and wider staff were strained.

His direct reports perceived him as a micromanager and felt hamstrung and not trusted to get on with their work. They were unsure where their jobs ended and his began.

When he discovered how he was perceived, Søren was shocked. While he thought he was being results focused and helpful, others experienced him as anxious and nitpicky.

It's absolutely no use if you see yourself as forthright, easy to understand, and approachable while others see you as blunt, self-centered, and frightening. When you see yourself as direct and others perceive you as a bully—you run into problems. You might be the smartest person in the room, but if people perceive you as boring, arrogant, or out of touch, they will reject you.

How on earth do we as leaders know if we are perceived the way we want to be? How might we shift unhelpful or inaccurate perceptions, or bridge the gap between how we see ourselves and how others see us? As a leader, knowing what others think of is you is important. Whom you take notice of in shaping your self-perception matters.

CASE STUDY: BANKING ON WOMEN

In the early 1990s, I was invited into a bank to work with a group of eleven women economists who felt invisible. They loved their work, knew they were capable, and mostly liked working for their managers. What was missing was any interest from their managers in them as people. Not one of them had feedback on the quality of their work. Managers would take their reports and proposals and present them to the government without giving them credit.

This was a group of intelligent, vibrant, and resourceful women. How might they learn how they were perceived? What was the best way for them to receive the recognition they craved? I decided to implement 360-degree feedback but feared that many would leave the organization once they had their results. I alerted the deputy chief executive who had contracted me. He said, "That's a risk I'm willing to take. I want these economists to flourish. Let's proceed."

The results came in. To their astonishment, the women discovered that their bosses, peers from other agencies, and staff rated them highly on most of the twenty-six items. I then led a program called Banking on Women. Within a year, seven of the women had left the bank for other agencies. One became parliamentary adviser to the Minister of Finance, another headed the international investment arm of Bain & Company, another led the government's transport strategy, and a fourth helped implement the banking system in newly established Kazakhstan. Knowing how others perceived them inspired these women to use their talents.

While these economists first believed their contributions were invisible, they realized that many others perceived their work positively, including their managers. They discovered three things:

- Their self-perception and perception of others coincided.
- They wanted to work for people who interacted with them as competent professionals.
- They themselves were responsible for acting on how others perceived them.

Self-Perception: The Ego

Freudian psychoanalytic theory identified the id, the ego, and the super-ego as part of personality theory. Popular notions of the ego are that your ego is that aspect of the self which is invested in *looking good*. Emerging leaders want to project a positive self-image and differentiate themselves from the crowd. An ego is threatened when there is information counter to the ego's positive identity. Unfavorable perceptions can bruise the leader's ego. This hurts. Leaders will defend their self-image with one or more of six typical defensive tactics:

- Walking away, escaping, going silent, or acquiescing
- Justifying, explaining, or making excuses
- Attacking or blaming
- Condemning or judging
- Using derision, sarcasm, or cynicism
- Lying or denying

One complication is that people sharing their perceptions can fall into the trap of being *overly empathetic*. They hesitate. They don't want to hurt anyone. They want to make things better. (We'll go into the this more in the next chapter.) They fudge things by

- Overly describing, explaining, and analyzing all the things they see.
- Raising far too many issues, so no one knows what is most important.
- Not saying the behavior and result they do want.

Another complication is that hearing someone's perception of you *feels* so personal. Because your self-image is threatened, it can feel like an attack. However, there is another aspect of the self, the genuine self. The genuine self knows what you really think and feel about things. The genuine self has its own insights, reflections, experiences, and perceptions, and the genuine self can accept others' perceptions.

Leaders who want to expand their self-knowledge are able to accept that they are imperfect. They know they have strengths *and* weaknesses. While what they hear might be unpleasant in the short term, they know it is helpful in the long run and use the information to decide how they will respond. Leaders with presence lead with their genuine self. Their ego self falls in the background once their genuine self comes to the fore.

The Opposite of Strong Ego Is Low Self-Esteem

Some leaders consistently

- Doubt themselves.
- Obsessively critique their actions and decisions.
- Project low self-esteem.

Their ego has not been built up, and they have a poor sense of themselves. One common result of this is a failure to communicate clearly. Such leaders discount the fact they are highly capable in many areas or else they wouldn't have been given the job. It is hard work being around leaders who are blind to their own abilities. These leaders bat away positive perceptions and bring everyone's attention to their shortcomings.

By looking at your own life as your leadership material, you can quickly discover what or who in your original family caused you to doubt yourself or be self-critical. The problem can then be solved by building an accurate sense of yourself and your capacities.

CASE STUDY: JILL

Jill's track record in leading and implementing large-scale organization change was exemplary. She had led both significant restructures and the development of shared services delivering to several organizations. Appreciated immensely by her staff and boss, Jill was a perfectionist. In our initial meeting, she confided in me that even though she knew people loved working with her, and she produced great results, she felt joyless. Her self-assessment was that while she was personable and purposeful in her interactions with her boss and staff, in large groups she felt cold. She didn't enjoy being in larger groups and she knew she was uninspiring. "Where did this come from?" I asked. Jill began her story. Her parents were prominent public figures and rarely available to her. To be noticed, Jill decided to excel in whatever she undertook. When she topped her grades at school, her parent's focused on what she hadn't done. Jill learned to give little value to her accomplishments and focus solely on what had to be done next.

In our work together, Jill realized that she was disregarding the positive affirmations of her boss and staff. She felt she had to do and give more.

When a close friend of Jill's unexpectedly died, she realized she had been behaving as if her work were the most important thing in her life. She sensed her relationship with her parents still influenced her drive in her work. Her insight was that she chose to listen to the internalized historic demands of her parents' criticisms instead of the here-and-now perceptions of the people around her.

What accounts for leaders' clinging to out-of-date expectations? Daniel Goleman's model of emotional intelligence for self-awareness and self-management gives us a framework. Jill was self-aware but she had yet to translate her awareness into self-management and her relationships. I have found that the role of the *empathetic companion* is essential for leaders to translate their insights to change behavior.

I *mirrored* Jill, saying, "You choose to listen to your parents' perception of you rather than those around you." Jill decided to choose new personal advisers to listen to.

In one of our group sessions, we role-played a scenario where she would speak at a full staff meeting. The scene was set with several hundred staff and her C-suite peers. Jill looked confident and professional as she walked onto the stage. When she spoke, she appeared wooden and uncertain. I invited her to reverse roles and be one of the staff. The staff member took up Jill's role, replicating her posture, gestures, tone, and some of her words. I interviewed Jill in the role of the staff member. "What do you notice about Jill?"

"She is wooden and formulaic." It's evident Jill's self-critic was well developed. Being critical is easy. I was aware Jill was also an astute observer, and there was likely to be more to her assessment of herself. I knew Jill knew that too. I asked, "What is your second take? What is she doing that is workable?"

In the role of staff member, Jill assessed herself as thoughtful, well prepared, and caring. When Jill returned to her own role, she looked out to the staff audience, her eyes softened. She began again. "I want to talk with you about what is coming up. We have some tough decisions ahead. I am confident we can get through this period. And it will be hard work. We have the skills and experience. And this will require something extra from every one of us." Leaving behind the role of the *wooden list memorizer*, Jill sifted her behavior to become the *clear terrain reader*, *personable expectation setter*, and *companionable encouraging journeywoman*. In experiencing herself through the eyes of others, Jill drew together her thinking, knowledge, and insights to learn to accept a new perception of herself. She warmed up to the task in front of her, and in doing so she was able to develop and maintain a positive connection with the staff group even though her message was tough. She knew she didn't have to be.

In identifying the origin of her self-critic and experiencing its effect from "others' perspective, Jill refreshed her self-perception. She accepted she was warm, well-regarded, and highly able. Jill later reported that talking from her heart rather than what she had memorized, she warmed to groups, and they to her. Her humor, experience, and goodwill came to the fore. Her self-critic fell away and her internal *you-can-do-this encourager* was evident.

Leaders who doubt themselves or are hard on themselves are likely to be perceived as:

- Quiet in meetings.
- Unwilling to share what they really think and feel on important matters.
- Pushing back in unhelpful ways.

- Defensive.
- Unavailable or invisible.

Developing Self-Perception

Gaining self-knowledge is a part of normal human development, and "know thyself" has been a commandment since the times of ancient Greece. Self-mastery is key to success in any field of work. Leaders daily face a myriad of competing priorities, and their capacity to prioritize their time and relationships determines their effectiveness. With this is in mind, how does one perceive oneself?

The same capacity that enables you to be in the everyday detail of the business *and* step back and take a long view helps you to develop self-perception. Your ability to participate in meetings *and* read the dynamics *and* consider future interventions is helpful.

I meet many leaders who have strong self-insight yet don't act on it. There is a gap between what they know about themselves and what they want to do about it. Herein lies the problem with feedback: feedback identifies areas for improvement yet rarely provides a link to your own source of *workable* solutions.

If you are someone who wants to have all the answers, you are likely to come up with a satisfactory solution. Many leaders find themselves stumbling across a *learning gap*. Learning gaps occur when nothing in your experience has prepared you to respond adequately to a given situation. Given that most of us aren't accurate fortune-tellers, we are likely to uncover a number of learning gaps in our lives. Leaders who thrive with learning gaps are curious and always are willing to admit "I don't know how to do this."

I'm reminded of a story my partner told me. His four-year-old daughter didn't want to go to school. Why? Because she didn't know how to read and write! Similarly, when leaders don't know something they think they should, they are thrown offtrack. The challenge of finding a way through the fog is daunting. I find that what works best with leaders is to ask, "How would you want to . . . ?" Almost always, leaders can let me know precisely how they would want to "be" in these situations. They have a vision for themselves. Naturally, they don't know the details. My response is, "I can help you." Every leader should be prepared to offer help to their staff when a development area is uncovered.

Another way to develop self-knowledge is to reverse roles. By doing this, you see yourself as others see you. Reversing roles is not merely a technique. Reversing roles is a learning method whereby you stand in the shoes of others and look at yourself to see yourself as others see you. By consciously seeing yourself through their eyes, you see new possibilities. Your self-knowledge expands as you become aware of how you react in specific situations. You interact as if you were the "other," from their perspective. Hidden behaviors and relationship subtleties can be displayed. How you proceed from there depends on the purpose of the exploration. Your leadership coach using participatory methods might:

- Invite you to coach yourself from the "other" perspective.
- Invite you to one side of the scene and have others reenact the interaction, for you to see yourself and your impact in action.
- Invite you to point out what is working and what could be enhanced.
- Invite others to model how they might respond as if they were in the specific setting.

The choice of intervention depends on the coach's assessment of how you learn and the outcome being sought.

Learning Methods That Work

It is simply impossible to change your behavior or expand your presence from reading a book or doing an online course. What works is learning new responses in your everyday interactions—in peer learning groups with participatory methods. Role-playing and replicating specific moments in here-and-now peer relationships can be helpful. Using the information gained from these sessions to brainstorm new directions and practice alternative behavior can result in great gains. Behavioral learning is neither intellectual nor theoretical. The role of the coach is to be a *companionable wise guide*, definitely not an *expert authority*.

CASE STUDY: MAX AND ROLE REVERSAL

Max is the CIO in a federal services agency. He is thoughtful, highly intelligent, and shy. He has a Ph.D. and twenty years' experience as a professor and experienced troubleshooter. His job is to lead and influence cross-agency collaboration in gathering big data that will be used to inform policy. In our group sessions, Max's conversation with both me and group members is focused on analyzing and musing on his observations of what was going on in the meetings he was in. His analysis of what is happening is accurate and astute. He doesn't act on this. I sensed Max would benefit by experiencing himself leading through the eyes of others. In our group session, we set a scene where Max was leading the cross-agency working meeting. There were competing and diverse views, forcefully presented. Max worked on his capacity to engage with people and make emotional connections. I encouraged Max to say what he was thinking. "We need to be doing this. . ." he says. His voice is quiet and he sounds doubtful as he talked with the group.

I invited Max to take the perspective of one of the CIOs to whom he was speaking. I asked a group member take up Max's position and to mirror Max's behavior: his body position, his tone, and some of his words. He did this. Max, in the role of CIO, looked surprised. Shocked even. Then thoughtful.

"What do you notice about Max?" I ask.

"He isn't very impactful."

"How might he be impactful?" I ask.

"He could speak louder. He could be more direct." Max returned to his own role in the scene. He leaned forward; his eyes lit up and his color increased. He increased the volume of his voice as he spoke to the group. He transformed from a *reflective analytical professor* to an *animated visionary and astute direction setter*. I noticed group members' vitality increased. Even in this role-play, they were engaged and taken aback by Max's impact. I said to group members, "Move your chair forward if you are drawn to what Max is saying and want to hear more." Every person moved their chair in. "Let Max know his impact on you." Group members shared their experience of him. Max now had the knowledge and felt experience of what enabled him to be more effective as a leader.

What creates this capacity for leaders to shift their behavior? Several processes come into play:

- A fresh perspective on yourself. You tap your own *refresh* button.
- Seeing and hearing yourself as others see and hear you expands your self-concept.
- Your self-awareness expands.
- A lingering self-doubt might be confirmed. You accept that yes, you are . . .

Mirroring and role reversal work best when there are trusted relationships among those involved. These methods are not for self-evaluation or criticism; their purpose is to expand your sense of yourself.

Shifting Perceptions

Every one of us has the capacity to influence the way others perceive us by shifting our behavior. The story of Antony gives us a useful example to work with.

CASE STUDY: ANTONY

Antony, a shy C-suite adviser, introduced himself to the group in the first training session. He is soft-spoken.

Take 1: "My job was in the Treasury, then I worked in several policy groups before heading to England for five years. There I worked in a local authority. When I came back, I picked up my current role as a strategic policy director." (I describe this as the "list" approach to introducing yourself. Based on a series of facts, there is little for audience members to connect with at any emotional level, and in most cases the leader is impersonal and not emotionally connected with him-or herself.)

I suggested to Antony that we take a readout of participants' responses. I invited them to bring their chairs closer if they were drawn to Antony and wanted to hear more, to stay where they were if they felt neutral, or to move their chairs back if they weren't drawn into what Antony had presented. Immediately, one person moved their chair back, two brought their chairs slightly forward, and the remainder stayed where they were. Their perception of Antony was that he was hesitant and a bit boring. Two said they wanted him to share something personal, something that was really *him*. Few wanted to continue a conversation with him.

Seeing people respond using movement has an impact, as do people's comments. I could see Antony warmed to the honesty of his peers' responses even though there were "negative" perceptions. He decided he wanted to do take 2. He looked at his peers and began again.

Take 2: "My first work role in Treasury taught me to contribute my ideas early in a group. We were working with economic policy, and I could see whoever spoke the loudest influenced. I moved to London and worked in a local authority for five years. I lived in a low-socioeconomic-status community and saw how our policies had direct impact on the social and economic lives of my neighbors. I saw how we could help people—which levers we could pull and which ones to ignore. I loved seeing the immediate impact of our work. Coming back home, I wanted to help make those changes on a national scale." There was a new response to Antony. Every person moved their chair forward. New responses were that he was perceived as thoughtful, pragmatic, and influential. People wanted to talk with him. "What levers did he work with? What made the biggest difference? What did he notice?" I noticed Antony was warm, friendly, and easygoing as he recalled his experience. He connected with his experience and to the group and vice versa.

As our senses "take in" the people and situations around us, our perceptions inform our thinking, knowledge, insights, foresight, intuition, and imagination. We learn more by sharing our perceptions with others. Often you will find that others have significantly different perspectives. Depending on the outcome you are looking for, you have a series of choices:

- Test your perception (guess) with others.
- Hold to your perception and alienate others.
- Persuade others to share your perception.
- Scan the implications of acting on your perception.
- Let your perception inform your stance on significant matters.
- Keep your perceptions to yourself.

While perceptions of others matter, rely on your self-validation. Avoid molding yourself to what others want you to be. Be prepared to disappoint people. You cannot be all things to all people. You have direct, personal, and ongoing access to your own leadership material. Let it define the genuine and distinctive you.

What do you do when you discover something unpleasant about yourself, something you wished weren't true? You might have learned that your temper, high standards, or intellect frightens others, or that people see you as critical or arrogant. Hearing these things can be a shock to anyone. Most leaders I know are embarrassed to hear something like this. They definitely wish it weren't true. Then what is to be done? Self-reflection is helpful. Ask yourself, What do I want to achieve here?

Looking back into your own life, ask yourself, Where did I learn this? What is happening now that has me respond in this way? What might account for this mismatch?

There Will Be Surprises

You see yourself as capable and effective, yet

- You miss out on a surefire appointment.
- Your manager gives you feedback that takes you by surprise.
- A customer or stakeholder complains.
- A staff member lodges a complaint.
- Peers avoid you.
- You are removed from a major assignment.
- You are seen to be closer to the stakeholder than your own organization.
- You champion your team at the expense of the organization.

Any one of these might cause you to reevaluate your approach. Leaders with strong peer relationships are more likely to be alerted when there is a perception mismatch.

There will be surprises. At some time in your career, you are likely to discover a gap in how you see yourself and how others see you. The only way to bridge it is to learn to read people and to read situations. The same practices that help you recognize invisible drivers will help you to figure out external perceptions. (See chapter 3.) When you are immersed in the hurly-burly of everyday work, taking time out for reflection is essential. The main thing here is to be willing to listen to others who are important to you. Then ask yourself, What do I want to do about this? And if you decide to act, How can I turn this around?

Developing Interpersonal Perception

Leaders with presence have a good sense of how others perceive them. They have tested their own perceptions, listened, learned from feedback, and practiced their abilities to read people. They trust their judgment.

Strengthening this ability can only be done by using your intuition, guessing, and testing your theories with people you trust.

Coming to Grips with Mixed Perceptions

I'm working with Chris. He looks and sounds like a leader. In our initial meeting, my experience of him is that he is forthright, intelligent, funny, open, and engaging. I sound him out on how he thinks he is perceived.

- *His negative self-perception report is that he is:* Not impactful, lacks vision, too tied up in details of his own business unit to attend to others, and "busy." He reports he is too quiet in meetings. He observes he is not working across the company.
- *Chris thinks his bosses' positive perceptions are:* Performing well. Delivering well in the business. Professional. Engaged. Doesn't bring the boss problems.
- *Negative perceptions from bosses:* Unengaged as a corporate citizen. Unavailable to others. Quiet in meetings.

What accounts for such mixed perceptions? Chris feels himself pulled in many directions. The context for Chris' development becomes apparent when he identifies his outcomes for executive presence:

- Being impactful.
- Leading with vision and drive to business forward.
- Easily creating trusted mutual connections.

In a group session with Chris, we set a scene: His team is discussing a technical problem. Chris wants to share his vision with the team. He begins. I notice he ignores what the team was discussing and begins talking about where he wants to take the business. All the time he is passionate, intense, and personable. I notice that his staff looked stunned. What might we do to come to grips with mixed perceptions?

I invite Chris to reverse roles with a group member. I ask the group member to take up Chris' role, his body position, tone, and some of his words. He does this. Chris is taken aback. He is watchful, then thoughtful. OK . . . I invite Chris to coach himself. In the role of staff member, Chris sees himself as out-of-step with his team and not taking them with him. He begins to come to grips with his staff's perception of him and how he might address this.

Often leaders are frustrated when they are perceived in different ways by different people. Bosses might look on them positively while peers or staff see them in other ways. This confuses them. Ultimately, being a leader means engaging in ongoing learning—encompassing and accepting a wide range of perceptions from others included.

Practice Session 4.1

How do you see yourself? Which four words best describe your positive perception of yourself?

- Capable
- Personable
- Trusted
- Results oriented
- Affirming
- Affiliative
- Productive
- Empathetic
- Intelligent
- Thoughtful

Practice Session 4.2: Interpersonal Perceptions

Make an assessment of how you think you are perceived now. Ensure you have at least five positive perceptions for every two or three not-so-positives.

Perceived by	Positive	Not So Positive
Federal/state government representatives, local government representatives		
Bosses		
Peers		
Direct reports		
Wider in your organization		
Stakeholders		
Other		

Summary

- If you want to help people, perception matters.
- Leaders with presence have a close match between their inner experience and how others perceive them.
- The genuine self knows what you really think and feel about things and has its own insights, reflections, experiences, and perceptions
- To expand your self-knowledge, accept your imperfections.
- Developing self-knowledge is a part of normal human development.
- While perceptions of others matter, rely on your self-validation.
- Leaders with strong peer relationships are likely to be alerted when there is a perception mismatch.
- Leaders with presence have a good sense of how others perceive them.

Chapter 5

Seeing the Mirror

THIS CHAPTER LOOKS AT ORGANIZATIONAL PROCESSES intended to expand leaders' self-knowledge and why these rarely work. It elaborates upon the concept of the mirror and the effect of accurate mirroring. This chapter also shows that traditional ways of giving "feedback" take leaders down the wrong track. More relevant than feedback is identifying the impact you have on others. This chapter concludes by debunking a few illogical and unhelpful organization learning processes and describing what helps leaders to truly change their behavior.

Building Self-Respect

Having confidence in your own abilities is core to self-respect. If you don't respect yourself, why would anyone respect you? When you accept and appreciate your capacities, you understand the value you add, and work becomes easier. Leaders with presence accept both their capacities and their frailties. They accept affirming comments and take them at face value, without questioning *why* someone would compliment them. They don't rely on others to let them know what they are doing well. If you want to monitor yourself on a challenging task, ask yourself, Have I done my best to . . .? or, What responses do I notice?

I've noticed that 360-degree feedback results rarely resonate with leaders, who can't make sense of what is being communicated or why.

One manager brought me his 360-degree feedback report, which had six pages of description of behaviors and four pages of suggested areas for development. Meanwhile his recent performance evaluation from his manager bore no relationship to the 360-degree report. He didn't know where to begin.

A second client from the same organization brought me his professional development plan. He had to choose two out of twelve competencies to develop in the upcoming year. "None of these are actually relevant to my job. I am not interested in any of these. I really want to learn how to write well in ways that make sense to people. Now that interests me."

What Do the Stats Tell Us?

When feedback is timely, personal, and put in context, people listen and act. How can we ensure there are people around us to let us know when we could step up and contribute more, or identify when we are inappropriate or have missed the mark? If we don't notice something is amiss, who would let us know? Who tells us when we are achieving and adding value? Your function as leader is to influence others. Accepting others' influence on you is essential. Deciding *who* you want to influence you takes thought and conscious choice.

Zenger and Folkman discovered that only half of leaders are comfortable giving positive feedback. It is no wonder many staff don't like feedback if they only hear about what isn't working. Further findings were:

- Ninety-four percent of feedback recipients said that corrective feedback improved their performance when presented well.
- Seventy-two percent said a leader can be most influential by "giving corrective feedback and advice when mistakes are made." These results are compelling. Not only are leaders who give good corrective feedback seen as influential; by doing so, they impact business results. The absence of feedback is interpreted by staff as a lack of interest. They feel overlooked and are left to make their own decisions on what to do and what is effective.

Human resources departments implementing 360-degree feedback tools frequently cut into the relationship between manager and staff rather than complement it. The feedback is often given by a professional unknown to the manager and unaware of either the organization's context or the manager's current development agenda. Why would anyone take what they say seriously?

Organizations who value productive working relationships between managers and staff are likely to have motivated staff. These managers and their staff are more likely to have conversations that matter to them both and to the results being produced.

Organizations that frequently restructure fracture existing relationships. Staff are less likely to trust their managers and are therefore less likely to listen to development feedback. Why would they? Their manager hardly knows them.

In a public survey conducted by Deloitte, more than 58 percent believed that their current management approach resulted in neither employee engagement nor high performance. What more of an indictment of performance management is needed?

The Demise of Feedback

Leaders can only serve as an effective mirror to others if they have mutual positive relationships, are present, and have empathy when communicating their expectations. This produces the best results, but most feedback is the opposite of this.

Arriving in the 1980s, 360-feedback was intended as a corrective to traditional one-way feedback, which took the form of directives from leaders to staff. This new kind of feedback was a chance for bosses, peers, and staff to anonymously share how they saw the leader along a number of parameters. The idea that staff could give feedback to their manager without fear of retribution was a revelation. Leaders ceased to be islands unto themselves and were given fresh reminders that the views of those around them mattered.

Here's how expectations of leaders changed for the better:

- Leaders were no longer seen as having "made it."
- Leading significant change required new approaches.
- Leaders as technical specialists gave way to leaders of people.
- Leaders decided what was to be done, while staff decided how.
- Leaders became coaches and developers of others.
- Leaders' personal capacities became as important as their skills and knowledge.

This type of feedback was a great concept; however, in practice it turned out rarely to be helpful. This is where feedback lost its power.

The Killer Elements of 360-Degree Feedback

- It's rarely personalized.
- It's rarely context related.
- It overlooks what the leader has developed.
- There are too many items.
- Bosses use it to avoid talking directly to their staff.
- Fearful staff rely on it to alert leaders to development areas.
- Results are filed and therefore not truly confidential.
- The results translator has little or no relationship with the recipient.

The reliance on formal systems to implement feedback misses the point. There is no one-size-fits-all solution. Contexts vary, and leaders' development goals are highly personalized. The choice of person delivering feedback and who makes that choice dramatically affects the leader's willingness to accept and act on it.

Feedback alone is not enough. Self-reflection is helpful, but it too is not enough. Leaders need a clear professional development path to respond to the areas they identify for their development.

Deciding who to involve in providing feedback becomes a political process when recipients know their feedback might well be considered by decisions makers in performance management, job applications, or career development. Ouch.

One benefit of 360-feedback is that it usually reveals new areas for development. But it can be a double-edged sword. I once attended a leadership program at the Center for Creative Leadership in the 1980s. I set goals, completed a 360-feedback tool, and filled out several psychometrics. The workshop itself included a "Looking Glass" business simulation, and further in-action feedback was given to us participants. The week was profound, and I learned a great deal. I came away with a long list of areas to develop and I had more on my plate than when I began.

Most leaders I know are acutely conscious of areas they want to develop to increase their effectiveness. In my leadership programs, I work with leaders' self-insight and their own interpersonal perceptions as they set outcomes for professional development. This way, their development occurs both within and subsequent to the program. They have either achieved the outcomes or are on their way to doing so when they conclude the program. They measure their success, knowing where they began.

Lead with What You Know

I work with many highly skilled and experienced leaders. Their feedback shows they excel in many areas and are *strong* in a myriad of competencies. Most 360-degree feedback, however, focuses almost exclusively on the areas to develop. They make this the main thing.

What is more important for leaders is to *accept* the capacities they do have, and relax and enjoy the results. When feedback tells them they are highly regarded, this is too often overlooked or assumed. Imagine the culture of our organizations if leaders accepted their strengths and truly enjoyed their work, rather than focusing and *working hard* on their weaknesses. In my mind, development areas require a fine-tuned approach.

CASE STUDY:

Merita had been told she was abrasive and annoyed people. She realized that she would purposefully dive into conversations without making firm positive connections with the person she was talking to. In our group sessions, others rapidly identified her as being *approachable* and a *trusted confidant*. Merita was astonished. She hadn't known she was perceived this way. She had focused on the perception she was abrasive. Over several weeks, she accepted this newfound knowledge. Knowing she was approachable and trusted, Merita shifted her approach when she wanted something. She became more personable with her requests, and her manager noticed she was more collegial. She became increasingly sought after for advice and guidance.

The Difficulty with Performance Feedback

The whole purpose of performance feedback is to open up conversations. How are you doing with what you set out to do? This is definitively evaluative. In ideal circumstances, getting together with your staff on a regular basis to look back and forward together has enormous value. In reality, however, given job changes, restructuring, and leaders' workloads, performance review and planning sessions are rarely carried out by people who know one another well. These meetings often end up being another chore to tick off. If the timing of performance reviews were not scheduled by the organization, most would not occur. Effective leaders do not rely on performance reviews. Instead they incorporate staff coaching and development into their everyday conversations.

Feedback from Managers Doesn't Work

Feedback is a great concept. Get the information, decide a course of action, and read the response—that's the theory. But what happens in practice? What kills the value of feedback?

- Staff don't respect their manager's perspective. "They don't understand what I do."
- There is no trusted relationship between the manager and staff.
- Most feedback focuses on what is wrong.
- Most feedback is evaluative.
- Behavior is described ambiguously or with long explanations and descriptions.

None of this works.

Never give feedback. It is the wrong strategy. Most feedback doesn't make sense. It is unhelpful to hear such critical remarks as "You do not speak clearly or concisely" or "You are too blunt, and people do not like it" or "You are overfamiliar with your staff." Recipients are none the wiser with what's expected or how to adjust their approach.

This kind of intellectual feedback might have a ring of truth, but so what? It does not help leaders understand precisely how they impact others. What alternative approaches are possible?

Unless there is an emergency, sudden and significant lasting behavior change is impossible. What is possible is for leaders to do three things:

1. Describe behavior imaginatively.
2. Describe the impact.
3. Describe what they want to happen.

If you are on the receiving end of the "development" feedback above:

- Appreciate the origin of the behavior.
- Define the new response you want to learn.
- Work with your manager or find a good coach.
- Find the origin of the behavior.
- Update the relationship between then and now.
- Generate new options for responding.
- Integrate your chosen option.

The "feedback" strategy that works for leaders is to develop relationships with your staff where you can talk about areas for improvement as a coach. Your role is to evaluate the self-awareness of your staff, help them expand their self-awareness, find out how they want to respond, and discover how you can help. Do this in ways that make clear to everyone you have their best interest at heart. Then having those crucial, awkward, essential conversations becomes second nature. It is impossible to build relationships based on criticism, no matter how accurate; instead cultivate relationships with positive recognition and perceptive appreciation.

How Do Leaders Learn?

Being mirrored helps us to see ourselves as others see us and helps build our self-knowledge. As my colleague Joan Daniels says, "If you spot it, you got it." This is the tricky thing. If you notice something in another person, like it or not, you are likely to share that trait as well. I found this knowledge unnerving. Early on, I'd spot something in someone, then keep it to myself because I didn't like knowing I had a similar behavior. I have found this principle encourages empathy when you are about to mirror someone. Think to yourself, If this were me, how would I want to hear this?

Mirroring itself is an early childhood stage of development. Caregivers who mimic and reflect a baby's expression and tone enable the baby to *see* themselves. The purpose of mirroring is to increase self-awareness, which occurs most effectively when there a positive connection between the *mirror* and the *receiver*. Where no positive connection exists, the mirror is unlikely to be accepted.

Shifting Gears

I notice many managers lose sleep the night prior to performance discussions with peers or their staff. They lack confidence that their feedback will be heard, accepted, understood, and acted on. Nail this, and you have invaluable relationships and greater productivity. Do this poorly, and your capacity for producing results through others fades. The main reason leaders fail to mirror well is that they overanalyze what is happening. They struggle to understand why their bosses, peers, or staff are behaving in a particular way. This is where they go down the wrong track.

Most leaders I know are astute analysts and perceptive readers of people, but analysis won't help you decide what to say, no matter how many hours of emotional angst you invest. Emotional angst comes from realizing if you offer your rational analysis of someone's behavior, they are likely to reject it. You imagine they might shout and storm off, and in all likelihood they will. This alone should serve as a warning that you are going down the wrong track.

Understanding why someone behaves in a particular way is unimportant, and second guessing is even less helpful. After all, this is not your business. What is important is what you as the leader will do about it.

When leaders shifts from analyzing and understanding to coaching and working alongside others, they shift into the territory of development conversations. This is the best approach for letting others know the impact of their behavior, be it positive or not.

Several principles apply for successful development conversations:

1. Expect that you could be the first person to raise this concern with the person. It may well be news to them. You may have spotted their blind spot.

2. If this is the first time anyone has raised the issue, he or she will need some time to digest the point. Expect your conversation to be one of several over a span of weeks, maybe longer.

3. Make a plan. Accurate mirroring may be sufficient for the individual to radically change their behavior, but they may be unwilling to change at all. Others may want to really understand the behavior and where it comes from. Here, adopting the role of coach is essential.

4. Most receivers won't know *how* to proceed. Leaders frequently respond by sending staff to training programs or finding them

a coach. Staff often don't fully comprehend why they are being sent or what they are supposed to achieve. Unless there is a clear relationship between the area of development, the outcomes the leader wants, and the outcomes of the program, this approach won't work. Leaders can instead ask, "How would you want to respond in this situation?" or "How can I help you."

Crossing the Line

Many leaders fear they are crossing a line by bringing a staff or colleague's attention to a development area. They hesitate and fret. I asked Robert what the line was for him. "The line appears when I'm not sure if the person is self-aware. I sense I might interfere in their psychology or stir up something from their background." This is true: You are going to stir something up. You are addressing a mismatch between your perceptions, the organization expectations, and the person's awareness of their effectiveness. What *right* do you have as a leader to do this?

When you consider the costs of staying quiet about your concerns, bring to mind the organizational costs of emotional energy spent navigating around that person, the results not being produced, and your own diverted attention. Imagine if this were you. Wouldn't you want to know if you were creating divisions in the leadership team? Or that your C-suite papers were rejected because they missed the mark? Or that you terrify your staff? How would you want a peer or boss to let you know?

A second line is drawn between what is supposedly personal and what is professional. Of course, this is sensitive. Most leaders don't mirror anyone other than their intimate confidants, partners, or children. While mirroring and doubling are essential for healthy child development, they are infrequently applied in organizations. That leaders cross this line between what is personal and what is work is essential. These are work interactions. Improved business results and positive work cultures depend on them.

There is a third line. In Johari's terms, leaders with presence frequently shift information from the psychological unknown into the known with staff and peers. They accept their mandate to shape culture and engender respect. The response to being "seen" might be embarrassment, shame, or anger. It can be painful for staff and peers to hear they are not perfect. Many people associate emotional pain with rejection or the loss of someone special. This is why associating performance evaluations with behavioral adjustments doesn't work.

Leaders don't want to cause others "pain," yet the cost to any business of not crossing this line is substantial, both reputational and in lost productivity. Reassurance of your confidence in their capacities and in your working relationship helps recipients disconnect from earlier negative experiences.

Leaders are more effective when they begin a conversation regarding someone's behavior with a question such as "Are you aware that . . .?" followed by "Do you want to know how that impacts me, or the team, or the task?" Savita is personable and committed to developing her staff. She begins her "performance conversations" with "I want to let you know something that will help you with your work. I want you to be successful. I want you to be more effective." Who could resist?

Crossing this line—the line between what is unknown to the recipient yet known to you and others—is like bringing the proverbial elephant into the room. What has been unspoken is now spoken. It won't be easy, but by doing so you will develop deeper emotional connections and stronger working relationships. If you believe emotions should be kept out of the workplace, you won't succeed in developing yourself or others.

Each of these lines, while invisible, is *felt* by both leaders and recipients. This third line especially can create a shock for the recipient. Sometimes the unknown becomes known not from self-discovery, but because another has noticed its impact on relationships or business results. It is the leader's role to address this, and their role to help staff develop a fresh response.

The Shock of Learning

Learning can come as a shock when it confirms a hazy suspicion or brings to light what others have been afraid to let you know. Your blind spot becomes obvious and begins to make sense as your self-awareness expands.

Recall our discussion of the learning gap. When uncovering a previously unknown issue, there is also an experience gap in how to approach the situation. Traits such as courage, grit, and curiosity will help people to deal with this discovery, and their choice of response can then be explored.

Most feedback is useless criticism. Formulaic approaches like the feedback sandwich (something positive, the real thing you want to say, then something positive) only help leaders when they lack confidence in their relationship with the recipient.

Who knows what is truly behind the behavior? You may find out, but it's ultimately unimportant. The main thing is to determine whether the person can accept what you are saying. Can you both maintain a positive relationship? And how can you help them turn their behavior around?

You will quickly discover whether there are misunderstandings or new expectations that have yet to be communicated. Will the person's "psychology" be damaged? Probably not. More damaging is malicious innuendo, unexpressed negative perceptions, doubts, aggressive criticism, and unclear expectations. These create paranoia.

How can someone be a leader while not knowing themselves well? Easily. It may be that no one has cared about them enough to let them know what's working with their approach and what is not. Or, no one has offered to help them develop new capacities.

CASE STUDY: BRIGIT

Brigit is a C-suite lawyer in her fifties who has neither been offered nor sought leadership development. She is not alone. Years of annual performance discussions have failed to touch on crucial areas. She and her managers both avoid them.

What can we do to ensure we have people around us to let us know when we are out of line, inappropriate, or missing the mark? If we can't work out for ourselves that something is amiss, who would let us know?

CASE STUDY: OLIVER AND THE MIRROR

Oliver and I are meeting for the first time. His manager wants him to have greater presence and be taken seriously by senior leaders. Oliver presents as personable yet shy. As he closes the door, he looks down, then at me, with his eyes closed. He makes an offhand, self-effacing remark. I feel awkward and I can see why senior leaders would, too. I become aware that Oliver is open and forthcoming. He has significant self-insight and talks without stopping, but I am unable to assess what is important. I let him know this. "Yes," he responds, "when I'm nervous, I talk a lot."

I can imagine this confuses senior leaders who prefer specific information and brief responses to their questions. I intervene. "Slow down. I can't concentrate. I don't know what you are saying. I don't know what the important thing is that you are telling me."

Oliver laughs. "Lots of people say that to me."

I continue. "I'm giving you something. I'm handing you an imaginary bag, and inside this bag are hundreds of pauses and I want you to use these. One for every sentence." Oliver laughs again.

Feedback in the moment works best when both parties have a trusting relationship.

Oliver's Story: Oliver had moved through his career with no real thought. His personal life, friends, and four children were of central importance to him, and he had not moved "up" in his career. At school, he was dyslexic, resulting in a lack of confidence. Oliver's own assessment was that he wasn't very bright. He had five friends throughout his schooling, all very intelligent and capable. He liked being part of this group, and his way of coping with his dyslexia was to make self-deprecating jokes. His school friendships had endured, and their families vacationed together. Each of his friends had strong professional identities: lawyer, doctor, eye specialist, architect, and accountant. Oliver remained blind to his own capabilities.

I ask Oliver what he wants to do. He says, "Grow up. I want to achieve results, have fun, and ensure people want to work together."

Oliver set three outcomes for greater presence:

- To get his head out of the grass, think further ahead and have a futuristic outlook.
- To speak to senior leaders with purpose and be perceived as a leader, not a joker.
- To operate competently and confidently in complex environments with bosses, stakeholders, and staff.

We agreed to measure success by:

- Remaining brief and concise.
- Dropping the throwaway comments.
- The frequency of senior leaders coming to him for advice.
- How often he was invited to take on new responsibilities.

The Four Criteria for Effective Mirroring

- It's immediate, personalized, and context related.
- There is a trusted, respectful relationship between giver and receiver.
- The mirror is simple and easy to understand and is tied to the leader's expectations.
- This is an ongoing conversation on how the receiver is developing.

Direct Is Best for Some

The worst and best mirrors I've received were direct and to the point. Each time they came from someone who was important to me and whom I respected.

"Are you aware you are talking to me as if I've asked you to chew on a dirty dishcloth?" But no, I wasn't!

"Do you realize how boring you are? You've been talking about this to me for over a year." Hmm. That was true.

"Don't you think you might be taking too much responsibility for *our* experience?" Yes, I knew I was.

I hated hearing those things. I also knew they were accurate. Did I like the mirroring? No, not at all. Am I still in strong relationships with my mirrors? Yes. All three remain close colleagues. Have my relationships improved? Significantly. Was my ego bruised? Definitely, in the short term. Has my self-awareness expanded? Substantially.

Notice in these examples that the "feedback" is not formulaic. These are peer interactions in which both parties assume an equal stance (even though one was my boss at the time). These three people noticed something in our relationship that wasn't working. I imagine each one

- Thought about how they wanted to bring this to my attention.
- Assumed it was their role to be direct.
- Expected more of me.

When specific behavior negatively impacts business results or productive cultures, then it's the leaders' function to act. This is not about correcting or criticizing people; it is about helping people increase their effectiveness as you enact your role as leader.

Practice Session 5.1: Build Self-Respect Daily

1. Write down six successes each day for the next month.
2. Write down one insight from today that increased your presence.
3. List six abilities you bring to your work.
4. List six qualities your close colleagues would use to describe your value.
5. List three things that distinguish you as a leader with presence.
6. What is one thing you will stop doing?
7. Who drains your energy? Who will you move to the outer circle in your life?

Summary

- Seeing yourself as others see you is an important part of psychological health.

- Seek out what others have been afraid to let you know.

- Traditional feedback has limited value. More relevant is knowing how others respond to you as a leader.

- Give up analyzing or understanding others' behavior; it won't help you to act.

- It is your function to act when specific behavior negatively impacts business results.

- The best results are produced by being present and having empathy when communicating your expectations to those around you.

Chapter 6

What Is Professional Development?

BECOMING AN INSPIRING LEADER requires a new approach to professional development. Our task as leaders is to expand our progressive roles: our capacities to build relationships, make decisions that have positive strategic outcomes, and produce results that matter. In this chapter I cover how leaders begin the shift from default to progressive behaviors. It also shows how to tap into new possibilities as you identify your development goals—even though you will have no idea at first how to achieve them.

Unless we are fortune-tellers, work continually throws up unplanned events. Leaders' capacities to respond productively are what creates their track record and reputation. Leaders with overdeveloped default behaviors create emotional churn. People might find them technically brilliant but dislike working with them.

Fear of conflict, lack of empathy, an inability to express themselves simply—all will trip them up. They need courage to recognize things aren't working and be willing to listen to trusted bosses, peers, and staff. By identifying new development goals, their curiosity is activated, their psychology and physiology are reordered, and they expand their presence.

How does professional development apply to us as leaders, and how might we measure the results? What might significant others notice? How do our personal capacities affect the bottom line?

We can begin to answer these questions by distinguishing between (1) professional skills and abilities and (2) personal skills and abilities.

Professional abilities include legal, financial, planning, marketing, medical, engineering, environmental, managerial, organizational, analytical, and social services skills and qualifications. Personal skills and abilities include listening, leading great meetings, developing trusted relationships, sharing vision, providing direction, allowing perceptions to surface, holding firm under fire, collaborating, speaking up, being curious, reading context, acting productively in volatile situations, and sorting out conflicts.

Are professional skills easier to learn than personal skills? The central thing here is that the learning processes for each are different. In this chapter, we will explore these differences in detail.

What Is Being Developed?

A 2016 survey of senior government leaders in New Zealand found that, overall, leaders are honest, courageous, goal focused and resilient, with a range of relative strengths. They

- Are strong in strategic thinking and planning.
- Demonstrate achievement, drive, and ambition, with a strong delivery focus.
- Are resilient and able to deliver hard messages.

However, several areas for development were identified:

- Forty-four percent of leaders struggled to communicate and lead in ways that inspire and convince others to follow.
- Forty percent needed to learn to delegate effectively.
- Forty percent had difficulty reading political drivers, providing free and frank advice, and developing effective relationships with political representatives.

While these leaders possessed many strengths that were helpful and desirable for their roles, the survey showed that their relationships and capacity to communicate in a range of situations have been compromised for want of skills and tools.

Why would this be? Were technical capabilities easier to teach or prioritized over *personal* capabilities? Were the learning methods being used out-of-date? Whatever it was, by focusing on developing skills, tools, and techniques, leaders' abilities to influence and inspire, read relationship drivers, and produce results through others were left behind.

These results are a sign that approaches to leadership development need to change. Teaching communicating, inspiring people, delegation, navigating drivers, and developing relationships as tools and techniques is the wrong approach. Being *taught* by experts doesn't work.

Relational capacities are best learned in peer groups guided by insightful experienced companions. Learning by experience, in live settings, through role-plays and scenarios and in here-and-now interactions with structured debriefs, works.

The central premise here is that leaders look to their own lives and relationships for leadership material rather than rely on external models, frameworks, and sources.

As we all know, engaging hearts and minds takes more than skills and information. Let's take the example of delegation. The principles of delegation have been known to leaders for years. They have definitions and steps. What helps leaders to delegate?

Delegation is not one-way, from leader to staff. Delegation is a relational process with at least two players involved. Great delegators ask for what they want, clearly describe the results they are looking for, and both agree timing and parameters of progress reports. The delegatee knows clearly what is expected and when, and who they can go to for help. Both can assess whether they have the capability or potential.

Leaders who prioritize staff development produce results. This approach enables leaders to assess their part in ensuring success. Every leader will have been on the receiving end of both inspired and poor delegations. They can learn from this.

Many of us have been asked to do things beyond our known capacities, resulting in great outcomes. The crucial element was being trusted by whoever asked us to undertake the task. We were given the freedom to rise to the occasion in how to deliver, or we were specifically coached. Without hearts and minds engaged there is little chance of an outcome beyond mechanical ritual.

Individuals learning through information and techniques no longer works. It's the wrong approach. Communicating, inspiring people, working through others, navigating drivers, and developing relationships can only be learned in groups. What *does* work is leaders learning in live settings, through role-plays and scenarios, in their here-and-now interactions, with structured debriefs. Individual leaders learn from how others experience them, not in intellectual isolation. The central premise is that leaders look to their own lives and relationships for their leadership material rather than rely on external models, frameworks, and sources.

Personal Development for Professional Success

How many times have you worked alongside a brilliant expert who gives good advice but burns people with their acerbic wit, harsh criticisms, and judgments? What about yourself? Might you alienate people when you are under pressure; express hostility in response to competing ideas; or alienate bosses, staff, or peers?

There is an illogical yet direct, predictable, and positive relationship between personal learning and professional success. Leaders who are unable or unwilling to work well with people incur substantial business costs. The time spent sorting out personal grievances takes focus away from leading, implementing strategy, and measuring impact. The emotional toll negatively affects organizational culture, engagement, reputation, and results.

Leaders can learn to listen, run productive meetings, empathize, give free and frank advice, *and* provide direction. Finding ways forward through conflict and difficulties is essential. Early in my career as a teacher, nothing in my training had prepared me to deal with students coming to school hungry or beaten, or how to respond when one student stabbed his older sister in the playground. My training had prepared me to create curriculum and teach lessons but did little to help me lead a thousand multicultural teenagers in a low socioeconomic community. What helped most were experienced teachers who showed me how to be in these settings and who encouraged me, coached me, and believed in me. I learned not to fear students when they were upset, hurt, or angry—more, I learned to intervene pragmatically, care, and listen.

How do leaders learn? How does anyone learn? The traditional approach to adult learning is too simplistic. Emphasizing information, technical skills, and content over behavior shortchanges leaders and diminishes their effectiveness. When people skills are thought of as "soft," "touchy-feely," or "illogical," behavioral learning is devalued. Thinking that skills and techniques preside over behavior and relationships is wrong. Behavioral learning is the key to leaders' success.

Slap-on-the face performance feedback, poor management, and sudden unexplained termination has left a sour taste in many mouths. These events result directly from leaders' inability to

- Read their environment.
- Intervene when people are working against the culture.
- Gain staff buy-in with shifts in direction.
- Assess capability implications of new directions.
- Develop peer relationships with people in authority over them.

Leaders, like anyone else, can learn from these experiences, which is why the systems scientist Peter Senge encouraged leaders to develop learning cultures in their organizations. Counter to this approach are organization-driven systems of performance management, "evidenced-based" evaluations, reviews, and restructures, which all stifle learning. With this book, I'm encouraging you to develop a personal learning culture.

Three Levels of Learning

By differentiating different types of learning, leaders can better know the lay of the land. How are these defined? In their work with Psychodrama

Australia, Peter Howie and Diz Synnot identify three levels of learning: tertiary, secondary, and primary.

Tertiary: Information and Knowledge

Our brains accept information and use it to record, recall, and think. Actively using our memories and applying information enables us to be subject matter experts. Information and knowledge is best taught through lectures, discussions, reading, podcasts, videos, and reflection. Each of these learning methods focuses on the learner as recipient. Using our memory, thinking, and intelligence, we thrive in evidenced-based environments.

Secondary: Skills, Tools, and Techniques

The brain's nervous system activates muscles in the body. Practice embeds patterns of movement and ways of doing things. Feedback loops indicate our level of skill. Skills, tools, and techniques are best learned through practice, discussion, demonstrations, simulations, on-the-job learning, critical reflection, and interactive dramatic methods. Learners interact with specialist teachers, coaches, and mentors.

By contextually applying knowledge and information, we develop our professional identities as doctors, marketers, IT specialists, business analysts, and leaders. Our capacity to explore, research, and judiciously apply our skills comes to the fore. Secondary learning applies to developing and implementing strategy, managing performance, selling, overseeing procurement, reporting results, and managing stakeholder relationships.

Primary: Behavior

Both neurobiological and physiological systems are activated. Physical movement, spatial awareness, and psychoemotional responses also play their part. Primary learning is illogical, irrational, emotional—and deeply relevant for today's world. It guides leaders to respond contextually and integrate their technical acumen with their vision, insights, experience, and intuition. This capacity enables leaders to navigate the complex and invisible mix of forces coming their way and respond relevantly.

Primary, or behavioral, learning comes from reflective discussions, writing, conversing with intimates, role reversal, examining worldviews, real-world interactive simulations, and self-reflection. Learners work as peers with trusted friends, colleagues, teachers, coaches, and mentors.

Experience, vision, intuition, emotions, responses, thinking, actions, and feeling

Ideas, information, knowledge, skills, tools, and techniques

context

FIGURE 6.1   Primary Learning Is Holistic

Behavioral learning is holistic and enhances our social capacities. It utilizes our intuition, experience, vision, and curiosity to integrate thinking, feeling, and action. Applying insights, reversing roles, having meaningful conversations, developing trusted relationships rapidly, acting on what is important, and responding relevantly are the results of behavioral learning.

To summarize:

- *Knowing* is tertiary and related to information about the world, life, and ideas.
- *Doing* is secondary and is about being able to do things.
- *Being* is the primary level and is related to who you are.

All three levels are relevant to our functioning as effective leaders in the world.

How important is tertiary and secondary learning for leaders? In one group session, I invited leaders to recall a time when they first realized they were a leader. I heard responses such as the following:

- "I was nine years old, helping in my father's fruit store, and I could see it needed to be organized. I saw that customers couldn't reach the fruit they wanted."

- "I was twenty and working in London, and I was asked to lead a team. I could see there were problems and I had ideas about what we could do."
- "I was asked to captain the football team. I wasn't particularly good at the sport, but I realized I had good relationships with everybody."

Notice that not one of these leaders was chosen for their skills or knowledge. They were chosen for their ideas, their ability to initiate action, or their relationships. Yet how many leaders are appointed after exhaustive psychometrics, simulations, and interviews? And how many of these executives fail to integrate with their teams and deliver?

Some of the best leaders I work with have varied professional backgrounds and experiences they have learned to capitalize on as leaders.

One is a self-deprecating insightful leader who has a law degree and experience as a psychiatric nurse aid. She inspires others with her vision of what is possible; creates alignment within organizations; and delivers to bosses, customers, and staff.

Another is a courageous former army captain who had negotiated security arrangements with Afghani village chiefs for the first democratic elections and solo-parented two young boys. He navigates complex forces as he leads the innovation group in a large financial services company.

People love working with these leaders. They feel understood and flourish under their encouragement, direction, and high expectations.

Yes, each of these leaders has significant knowledge and skills. What makes them exceptional is how their life experience is reflected in their humanity and personal qualities. They know their role is to provide encouragement, vision, and direction, and they actively intervene when they see people working against their or the company's vision. Because of their relationships, staff and peers know where they stand with them and produce results.

The illusion that a leader's personal life is separate from their professional life creates a false sense of identity, as their capacity to learn from their experience is overlooked. Early educators used the "nature or nurture" paradigm for understanding our capacity to learn. Leadership theorists ask, "Are leaders born or made?" What is now apparent is that such one-dimensional perspectives are inadequate paradigms to have conversations on how leaders learn.

Making Relationships Visible

Leaders with presence have strong interpersonal and group skills that contribute to positive working cultures and great results. They understand mutuality in relationships, that relationships are two-way. They understand the value they bring to relationships and they know what others want from them. They can see things from others' perspectives. They know what they want to achieve but might not know how. Leaders with presence accept that they cannot know everything. They are not perfect; however, they are genuine. They begin every interaction with a clear, mutually beneficial outcome in mind.

What makes one leader visible and another invisible? Relationships are invisible, yet *how* leaders behave significantly impacts those around them and how they produce results.

There are many ways of making relationships visible using representational methods. Firstly, we can use distance as a "measure" of any relationship. Using a simple picture of two entities, as in the diagram below, we can depict a relationship by assigning meaning to the distance and the direction of the arrow.

FIGURE 6.2 Making Relationships Visible

The distance between the two circles can reflect the importance of the relationship, frequency of interactions, or trust. The density of the line can represent intensity of the relationship, weak or strong. In figure 6.2, it is apparent the relationship between Jim and his team is both important and one-way. By making the relationship visible, Jim can assess whether his relationship with his team is fit-for-purpose or requires attention.

Secondly, leaders can use physical continuums to bring visibility to and explore diverse views on controversial decisions. The two ends of the topic are marked out, and participants "take a position" standing on the line. When asked, "What prompts you to take this position?" everyone can both see and hear where they stand, both on the issue and in relation to one another. Making their position visible communicates more broadly than words. One impact is that people feel and act on their inclination to move toward or farther away as others express their views. The discussion is no longer theoretical but has vitality as people move in response to hearing and seeing one another's positions. Everyone in the discussion has the same information and knows the range of influences in the group. The experience of the spatial impact of their own and one another's positions activates more of the leaders' thoughtful capacities with their experience. They truly "engage."

There are several options for clarifying similarities and differences. Three include:

- Have people at different parts of the continuum say what is behind their position.
- Propose people get together with someone who has a different position from them and share views.
- Propose people who have similar views get together.

Leaders can bring visibility to what's happening in their discussions. Diverse views on any decision or issue can be displayed and explored. By taking a position on a continuum (figure 6.3), you can clarify similarities and differences within the organization.

FIGURE 6.3 Continuum Displaying Diverse Views

Physically taking a position and simultaneously seeing where others stand in relation to them and the issue enables leaders to rapidly clarify their thinking.

A three-dimensional way of exploring differing viewpoints is the sociogram (figure 6.4). Typically, a leader expresses their vision and others take a position in response. In a group exercise, the leader might stand at a central point or place a chair there to represent their vision. Using distance as a measure of closeness, others take a position reflecting their response.

By asking questions such as "What brings you close to the vision?" "What accounts for the distance?" or "What would bring you closer?" everyone can hear the range of views within the group. As people influence one another, their new position on the topic is visible.

The leader facilitating the group is an integral part of the discussion and not a removed observer. Conversations conducted via continuums and sociograms enable participants to share their experience, intuition, and intelligence. Each person knows where they stand in relation to others. They are in primary learning territory compared to round-table conversations, which are more frequently secondary or tertiary.

As they influence one another, leaders move to display their new position on the matter in hand. This is classic "learning on the job"—primary learning, where all the leader's experience is relationally engaged.

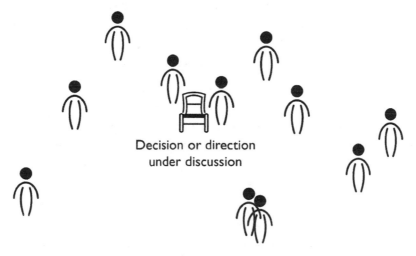

Decision or direction
under discussion

FIGURE 6.4 Leaders Exploring Diverse Views

CASE STUDY: JIM

Jim knew his team meetings were flat. He wanted his team to participate, yet they were silent. Listening in, I became aware that his voice
was loud—so loud it felt like being out in a hail storm. "Are you aware
your voice is loud?"

"Oh, yes," Jim said, "Everyone tells me that."

I hesitated and then took another step. "Do you want to know its
impact on me?" Jim went quiet and looked at me warily. I knew this was
a special moment: I might have been the first person to say this to him. I
swallowed, then said, "I can't concentrate, and I can't think. I sense you are
the authority on this matter and probably won't want to hear from me."

A look of dismay came over his face, then one of understanding.
Something was making sense. Jim and I discussed where he learned to
speak so loudly. Growing up among twenty cousins, he had learned to
shout to be heard. He was about to adjust.

Jim might be described as a *voluble determined broadcaster*. He realized that speaking like this meant that his team members were most
likely to react as *stunned watchful mutes*. Jim and I discussed several
options he could take to encourage participation. He chose to work on
becoming a *curious explorer and listener*. We tried again, and he said, "This
is a problem we have, and this is the outcome I want. What might we do
to resolve it? Let's hear one idea from each of you. Then we can decide
what to do next." With these two shifts in his behavior—lowering the
volume of his voice and becoming curious—progress could be made.

By displaying relationships diagrammatically we have a powerful representational tool. This helps us to discover our impact on others.

Increasing Your Visibility

There are many ways to increase your visibility as a leader. Visible leaders
participate and contribute and have a wide network of relationships. They

know their reputation precedes them. Those around them know how they feel and what they think on important matters. They have a reputation for approachability and contributing to business goals.

On the other hand, being silent in groups or contributing rarely ensures you remain "invisible." Others cannot know what you think and feel.

A second way leaders can increase their visibility is to form more relationships and increase their emotional expansiveness, allowing them to relate easily to large numbers of people. (See chapter 3.) To increase your emotional expansiveness, put your hand up for challenging assignments, use social media, introduce yourself to people, share something about yourself, and ask simple questions such as "What's on your agenda today?" or "What captured your attention in this session?" Be genuinely interested in those you meet.

> **To inspire:** *To make someone feel that they want to do something and that they can do it*
>
> *To give (someone) an idea about what to do or create*
>
> *To fill (someone) with the urge or ability to do or feel something, especially to do something creative*

How do leaders inspire others? They have many ways. Those I know have one or more of these attributes. They:

- Help people and ask for help.
- Believe people are capable.
- Share their vision and encourage others to share theirs.
- Share their ideas and are curious about others' ideas.
- Are accessible, inclusive, appreciative, decisive, and selective.
- Run great meetings; love being in groups; are tuned to feel, see, then tame the elephants.
- Find pathways among conflicts and differences in groups.
- Help people make connections with one another.

- Create and belong to communities.
- Get things done.
- Are trusted and have tough conversations.
- Let people know how they think and feel about things.
- Hold confidences.

If these "attributes" could be learned, secondary and tertiary learning methods would work. However, these are attributes derived from leaders who connect emotionally with others. They understand what people need to succeed. They can learn this by understanding themselves and how they currently impact others, and making adjustments.

Behavioral learning is governed by a series of nine principles.

1. Outcomes are highly personalized, context related, and describe a future state.
2. Responsibility is shared with two or three specifically chosen peers and/or bosses within the organization who provide oversight. Failure to provide this element limits implementation.
3. Trust is built within a system of peer companions who invest in authentic relating.
4. A holistic approach in a participatory experiential learning setting increases reflection, insight, and broader areas of application.
5. The here and now, in-the-moment experiences of leaders greatly impacts and informs what works and what doesn't.
6. Leaders choose their new behavior to reflect their genuine self, and not a constructed persona.
7. Behavioral learning is implemented by the leader integrating his or her thinking, feeling, and action. This takes time to embed.
8. Clear success measures assists the leader to read the responses of others.
9. The coaching relationship is experienced as *insightful trusted companionship* rather than expert teaching.

Generating New Approaches to Old Situations

I use role-plays in my work. My clients love them because they replicate real-world situations. The setting can be historic, current or anticipated. The purpose, scene setting, and script are entirely derived from the client's experience, perceptions, and the outcomes being sought. Their peers take up the behaviors of the key players and rapidly replicate the dynamic moment where the protagonist wants greater presence. Depending on how the protagonist learns, several options for proceeding become apparent. Three of these are:

- Mirroring: The client and coach stand to one side of the scene and observe as two or three group members enact precisely what they saw the protagonist do. They mirror body posture, tone, and some of the words. The protagonist's insight into the situation broadens.
- Role reversal: The protagonist and a group member reverse roles. The scene is reenacted and the protagonist experiences the other's perspective. In seeing themselves as others see them, they expand their perspective.
- Modeling: Group members are invited to enact what they might do in this situation, or what they would love to do and would not dare to in real life.

Each approach expands the protagonist's insights and perceptions of the situation. It activates fresh thinking and generates curiosity with what might work for the group in their situation. They work from their experience, their context, their insight and tap into fresh approaches to what might previously have stymied them. The principle here is that none of these approaches is evaluative. Their purpose is for protagonist and group members to gain perspective and insight, decide the way forward themselves, and expand their capacities.

Embedding Learning and New Behaviors

Memory alone is insufficient for generating new behaviors. *Remember to smile. Look at people you are talking to.* Remembering to act in particular ways is tiring. The holistic nature of primary learning means you can trust your new response will emerge. A conscious decision to act "differently" is not required. What *is* required is your awareness of the situations you are in, trusting yourself, noticing yourself respond in new ways, and reflecting on the new responses you get. Several learning tools are helpful, such as identifying success indicators, using accountability trackers and behavioral metaphors, and being aware of progressive behavioral descriptions. The next chapter covers these in detail.

Practice Session 6.1: What Are Your Development Outcomes?

What new capacities do you want to have in the next eighteen months? What personal qualities would better influence and enhance your company?
How do you want to be perceived by others?
Write down three outcomes you want from leadership development.

1. _____
2. _____
3. _____

Practice Session 6.2: Broadening Perspectives on an Originating Event

Do this with a trusted friend or colleague.

- Briefly describe the originating event. How old were you? Who was involved, and what was happening? What residual feelings were you left with?

- Looking back, if you knew then what you know now:
  a. Which original *significant others* would you want to have had with you?
  b. What would you want to let each know?
  c. Specifically, who would you have wanted to comfort you at the time?
  d. Imagine letting your family know was happening. What would you ask the family for?

  Think of the current triggers for your default behavior. Briefly describe what is happening and who is involved.
- What are your feelings about the situation? Who around you really understands what happened?
- Who do you want to really understand what happened?
- In an ideal world, what would you have wanted to say or do?
- What would you have wanted your manager/peer/staff/other to say?
- What would you want your manager to know?
- What could your manager have done to help you maintain equilibrium?
- What insights do you have after completing this exercise?

Practice Session 6.3

Invite three people you trust to help with this next part. Have each of them ask you this question: "If you were to give some thought to how you would want to respond in this situation, what might it be?" If your answer is "I don't know," have a second thought, or a guess, and go with whatever comes to mind. What insights does this exercise provoke?

Summary

- Leaders' capacities to respond relevantly to challenging events, maintain relationships, and produce results create their track record and reputation.

- Leaders with overdeveloped default behaviors create emotional churn. People dislike working with them.
- Leaders who are unable or unwilling to work well with people affect their organization's culture, engagement, and results.
- The leader's mandate is to find ways forward through conflict and difficulties.
- Real learning is illogical, irrational, and emotional.
- Behavioral learning uses our responses, intuition, experience, vision, and curiosity to integrate thinking, feeling, and action.
- When people feel understood and accepted, they flourish.
- Identify goals and outcome statements as if they are your future state.
- Taking ownership of how you are perceived, and daring to consider how you want to be perceived, unleash your capacity to inspire others.
- Leaders understand the value they bring to relationships and what others want from them.
- Leaders with presence function as peers with their bosses, staff, and colleagues.

Chapter 7

The Fine Art of Identifying Outcomes and Success Measures

I T'S NOT ENOUGH TO LEARN NEW THINGS; you need to know how
well you have successfully implemented them. This chapter outlines
how to establish valuable personal outcomes and organizational success
measures. It also helps you identify personal indicators that reflect your
executive presence *and* ensure organization value.

How do we measure executive presence? Is it possible? How do we
know when we have expanded our capacities as leaders? How do we know
we are applying what we have learned in our organizations? What metrics
are essential to leaders' success?

How do you know when you have arrived anywhere? A list of goals or
outcomes ultimately is not enough. What do you measure to prove that
value is being added to your work?

Say you have a goal to go to Paris. How do you know you have reached
your destination? How do you know the trip has been successful? You
know Paris is x miles from your city and that if you are in Rue de Rivoli,
you are where you should be. You have achieved your goal. Was your
experience in Paris truly what you wanted it to be?

What were the signs of success of this trip? Might you have loved a
meal in a French café, watching Parisians going about daily life? Might
you have been inspired by the architecture of the apartments in Place des

Vosges, with their roofs one-third of the height of each building and their wrought iron balconies aligned? Or have you been uplifted by hearing the spontaneous orchestra setting up in the Republic Metro corridors? Might you have been touched by the exhausted young woman, baby on her hip, dropping you a note on the train, asking for money?

In achieving your goal of going to Paris, your experience has been expanded. Your senses are engaged, your thinking deepens, your feelings mingle, your imagination is activated, and your resourcefulness expands. This chapter is about identifying outcomes and inspiring success indicators for your leadership development.

With executive presence, you need to know when your desired outcomes have been achieved. In this chapter, you will learn how to identify indicators that ensure you are on the right path. We then look at how to measure success. By differentiating personal and organizational metrics, you will know whether your organization is getting the results you want.

Three Goals Are Enough

Goal setting is the mechanism to link personal development to professional success. Tempting as it might be to pursue a myriad of development goals, if leaders set more than three, they find themselves torn in too many directions.

Effective goals are outcome statements describing the desired future state as if it were current.

However, there is a prior step and that is to identify your *own* perceptions of how others experience you. There are two aspects to this: (1) your perceptions of others' positive perceptions of you, and (2) your perceptions of their negative perceptions of you.

Set within your current context, your self-knowledge together with your self-insight are the essential foundations for you to envision your future state—your learning outcomes become apparent.

The capacity to see yourself as others see you is called interpersonal perception. Developing interpersonal perception requires you to form your *own* view of your strengths and weaknesses by considering feedback together with specific comments from significant others and your own experience of your relationships. In taking ownership of how you are perceived, and daring to consider how you want to be perceived, you tap into your capacity for inspiration. Setting outcomes for leadership development is now relevant and grounded in this ongoing context.

There are four elements for workable outcomes:

- Your organization's context and key deliverables
- Your own context and deliverables
- Your acceptance of how others perceive your awareness of others
- Your description of how you want to be.

Leaders' Typical Executive Presence Outcomes

If you have identified outcomes for executive presence, you already have a vision for yourself. Thinking of your desired future state in the here and now creates excitement and possibility. Outcomes are results oriented rather than action oriented.

Once you accept this is the current state of your personal and organizational context, you can then look out into the future. The practice of setting outcomes serves multiple purposes for leaders; they can

- Accept they are visionary.
- Communicate outcomes simply.
- Project themselves into the future.
- See links between strategy and outcomes.

- Inspire others with their personal commitment.

Setting outcomes requires specificity. I don't accept ill-defined outcomes such as "have greater confidence." Instead, ask, What would I be doing if I had greater confidence? Who would notice? What would they be seeing me do?

Below are a few examples taken from leaders in the process of uncovering specific overdeveloped default behaviors. Each one is highly competent yet lacks confidence or empathy; they have significant capacities yet aren't using them or have forgotten they have them.

- Oliver becomes tongue-tied, verbose, or self-deprecating when he is with senior leaders. They don't take him seriously and question his abilities. He sets an outcome: *I am clear and concise with senior leaders.*

- Bosses notice Nick is quiet in C-suite meetings. Shy and the youngest in his leadership team, he speaks only when asked and retreats when colleagues push back. *Bosses, peers, and staff perceive me as calm, collected, decisive, thoughtful, authoritative, and compelling in groups.*

- Katrina is a troubleshooter and speaks only from her formal role. Her desired outcome: *People listen to me because they want to, not because they have to.*

- Kerry, while innovative and able, has lost her confidence after a setback. Her outcome: *To be known and respected as a collaborator who can bring people together to solve big problems.*

- Brad is talented and forthright but abrasive under pressure. He sets an outcome: *I am perceived as helpful, valuable, personable, knowledgeable, collegial, and collaborative. People want to work with me.*

- Maria is friendly and competent but also reserved and easily stressed. Her outcome: *People are inspired and motivated when I share my goals, expectations, and vision.*

- Rose is passionate, but she gets frustrated and competitive in C-suite meetings. Her outcome: *I maintain passion without overcrowding or overpowering my peers.*
- Bill is frustrated and goes silent when under fire from peers and senior leaders. His outcome: *To be known for finding ways through past conflict and enhancing positive working relationships among the players.*

Powerful development outcomes are desired future results stated as if they are already in place.

By imagining going beyond what you already know, you have immediately begun to embed the expansions of your capabilities. By imagining fresh possibilities, you are in new territory. Things that once held you back or tripped you up are no longer in the front of your mind.

Behavioral change takes time. Early in my career, I asked a psychiatrist how long it takes for someone's behavior to change. Of course, the question had some relevance to my own life: I was in a failing relationship at the time and wondered if I would leave or stay and make it work. He said it takes about seven years. I looked at him in shock and found it hard to believe, wishing it weren't true. His words helped me decide to end the relationship. There was no way I was going to wait seven years, and I had worked out for myself there was no guarantee the other person would change. However, I had ideas about the quality of relationship I wanted to have and set a series of indicators. Seeing the results from my own life, I applied this approach to my work with clients.

Once leaders recognize the impact of their default behaviors and decide on a new approach, they can choose indicators to let them know if they are on track. By choosing three or four simple indicators, it is easy for leaders to see the results of shifting their behavior. Immediate results will become apparent; however, it takes months for any new behavior to be fully integrated.

CASE STUDY: RIA

Ria works with a group of GMs, all more senior than she. Their brief is to reduce costs of purchasing internal services. In meetings, she is quiet and cannot think of anything to contribute. In our practice session, Ria role-plays talking to the GMs. She closes her eyes, then looks up to the ceiling. She tosses her head and carefully tucks her hair behind one ear. Occasionally she looks at the floor. Group members look uncomfortable even though they are in "role." I have no idea why she acts this way, but the exact reasons are not important for me to know. What is important is her relationship with the GMs. I sense that group members might see her as "arrogant"; I guess Ria herself might be shy.

I have a trusted relationship with Ria and others in the group, who are warmed up to assist one another in the learning environment. I ask group members to mirror one facial expression they noticed as she spoke. Three immediately look up to the ceiling, four look to the floor. Ria burst out laughing and covered her face with her hands. "I know. I look up and I look down. But I'm thinking."

I assess Ria has isolated herself from the group. She is in her own world. Leaders remaining connected with those around them when they are under pressure is a fundamental for executive presence. Rather than make a critique or give advice, the principle here is that group members have a response from their experience of Ria.

"I know you are thinking," I respond. "But ask a few people how they feel when you do this."

One replies: "I feel cut off from you."

Another adds: "The connection you and I had is lost."

"How about you look at group members and think while you are looking at them," I suggest. Ria laughs. She feels shy and awkward and this is a moment of group intimacy. Ria has learned something about herself with her peers. Will she dare to try something new in the group?

When you look directly at people, you give them a window into your genuine self. By closing her eyes, Ria becomes an island, safe in her private thoughtfulness but removed from the group. She learned this as a child—to shut out any moment she felt unsafe. By looking at group members and being aware of their warmth toward her, she travels to new territory. Accepting the human desire for connection can take effort for leaders, and influencing others is no mere intellectual exercise.

Ria tries again. As she talks to the group, she faces them. She pauses and thinks. Group members are aware of her thoughtfulness. She looks up and succinctly shares her experience and insights. Ria invites everyone to apply what she has said to their current situation, and they appreciate her experience and perceptiveness. They see her applying her intelligence and making her experience relevant to the group's agenda. The group discusses the impacts of businesses purchasing their services, the resulting loss of administrative staff, and the implications on their capacities to deliver. The discussion is lively and worthwhile. The group picks up on Ria's insight and direction, and she is delighted to add value with her experience and make a positive impact. She laughs, "I so don't need to be the ice queen anymore." She has chosen her first success indicator: *I look at people when I am thinking and when I am talking with them.*

This indicator looks deceptively simple. It has several functions.

- To keep Ria on the front foot with the program outcomes
- To generate progress toward her specific outcomes
- To capture and implement her experience of what worked for her

---

Substantial benefits result for organizations from the combination of leaders visionary outcomes and the simple, practical success indicators they choose. When leaders get the responses they want by behaving differently, their confidence increases. Knowing they are on track to achieving desired outcomes has significant benefits. They apply their learning in broader contexts and make bold decisions, knowing the likely impact and that people are confident in their judgment.

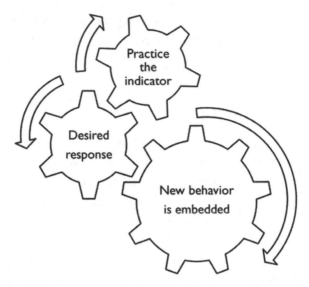

FIGURE 7.1   Process for Embedding New Behavior

How Do You Measure Success in Leadership Development?

How do you know when you have arrived? What is the impact on the organization of leadership development? Are leaders more likely to be confident in their relationships? How likely are they to have productive conversations? Would they remain formulaic in their approach? What enables the organization to shift to the real agenda?

New capacities become apparent when leaders learn to influence through their relationships:

- Staff engage and feel valued.
- Complaints from customers and stakeholders are responded to effectively.
- Performance increases.

Working through relationships rather than avoiding them means that expensive and distracting reviews, restructures, and investigations are resorted to less frequently. Leaders are able to listen to complaints and respond in ways people feel heard and valued. Leaders who engage meaningfully with aggrieved parties move things forward rather than defaulting to bureaucratic or short-term solutions. They use their capacities for relationships for the benefit of their agency and the aggrieved. Rather than looking at success in one way only, success parameters expand to include results *and* the quality of relationships.

Leaders with presence not only get done what is currently on the agenda, they actually shift the organization agenda to the things that really matter. The goals and results for the organization grow as leaders reach out in new and better directions. There is a clarity and confidence among the leaders and their staff, who share greater faith in the collective effort.

CASE STUDY: KATE

Kate leads the strategy group in a large government agency. At the beginning of our work, she clarified her primary outcome: "With conflict, I want to push back with senior leaders in ways that they want to work with me, I am trusted, I understand their needs, and I drive outcomes that work for everyone."

After some time had passed, we reviewed her progress. Kate reported, "I was running our strategy past the four deputy chief executives on the governance group. We had spotted some major roadblocks, and I wanted the governance group's view on what we had come up with. They simply endorsed what we had done. I was disappointed. I said, 'I'm going to push back here. I want to hear your take on our approach to the roadblocks. What else we might consider?'"

Surprised and delighted, the governance group sat up. Kate wanted their experience and expertise, not just a box ticked. A lively discussion ensued. Kate's capacity for "conflict" expanded with her desire to engage and access the abilities of senior leaders and achieve a better result.

Identifying Personal Metrics for Presence

Once outcomes are established, leaders decide upon their personal metrics for success.

Typical metrics related to gaining visibility include:

- Senior leaders seek me out for advice and input.
- Leaders invite me to lead cross-department projects.
- I contribute early in group settings.

To assess the impact of your new behaviors over several weeks, I advocate choosing two or three indicators and then tracking your progress.

Typical metrics related to influencing others include:

- I use "I" statements with my peers in leadership meetings and presentations.
- I help set the C-suite agenda.
- I look at others when I am thinking and talking.
- I speak in short sentences and pause between sentences.

These indicators fall into two categories. Some are actions the leader undertakes; others are observable results from their actions. Both approaches work. The essence of a good personal indicator is that others can notice visible results.

When leaders experience positive responses, their delight and sense of achievement reinforces the new behavior. Naturally, as they repeat the new approach, the behavior becomes embedded (see figure 7.1).

Of course, you will be drawn back into old ways of doing things. What is required is grit, thoughtfulness, and determination. If a leader says to me, "I don't feel comfortable with conflict," my response is, "Comfort is not the paradigm that works with senior leaders." By accepting the fact that discomfort comes with the territory, leaders can generate new responses. Old behaviors are often masked social behaviors that have no place in the workplace. These include obsessive apologizing, not wanting to "hurt" people with the "truth," and excessive friendliness and concern rather than attending to the work agenda.

The Success Indicator Tracker

How do you embed new behavior and remain conscious of your new approach? Identifying personal success indicators shows you the path—but the only way forward is through practice. It is best to have three goals for developing your leadership presence and three success indicators for tracking your progress. Any more than that and you will be pulled in too many directions and forced to resort to using your memory. Memorizing what you want to practice leads to failure, as even simple things get lost in the myriad of everyday events. Learning by memory is learning by rote, which will sap you of your vitality.

There are two approaches for measuring and tracking progress that are proven to work on a practical basis. The first one was developed along with my colleague Cher Williscroft. We use this with leaders as a monthly progress review of their chosen indicators. Cher and I established four measures:

- Improving
- Getting worse
- No change, and that's a good thing
- No change, and that's not good

The tracker is shown in the figure below.

Scoring	↑ up—improving; ↓ down—getting worse; ☺ no change—good; ☹ no change—bad; ? don't know/hasn't been tested											
Indicators	**Aug**	**Sept**	**Oct**	**Nov**	**Dec**	**Jan**	**Feb**	**Mar**	**Apr**	**May**	**June**	**July**
I use "I" statements with peers and bosses.												
I speak succinctly and pause between sentences.												
I contribute early in groups.												

FIGURE 7.2   The Success Indicator Tracker

What Makes This Work?

Being accountable and reporting results is an age-old mechanism. It works. This success indicator tracker works because in being accountable, each person asks themselves on a monthly basis, How am I doing with what I set out to do? What am I noticing? How are others responding to my use of 'I' statements?

Responding to these questions wakes you up. You become alert as you focus on the impact you make on people and as you learn to read situations accurately. I find after a few months, most people make significant progress in embedding their new behaviors.

Marshall Goldsmith takes another, equally effective approach.[1] He recommends daily tracking using a simple spreadsheet listing several indicators. He recommends only one measure: Have I done my best today to . . . ? Clients send me their spreadsheets weekly, together with their

---

[1] Goldsmith, *Triggers*, 124.

reflections on what they are learning. This intense and repetitive focus also helps embed new behaviors.

Simple Shifts Have Powerful Impacts

Remember that simple shifts in behavior will have immediate and powerful impacts. Below are a few indicators you might choose to measure:

- Looking at people when you speak to them
- Pausing between sentences
- Saying hello and introducing yourself to new people
- Being deliberate with when to contribute and when not to
- Using "I want" when you want something: "I want this by the end of today."
- Saying no without an explanation
- Saying "That's not possible" to impossible requests
- Saying what you want to say simply and succinctly
- Inviting involvement: "What are your thoughts?"
- Letting people know you appreciate them
- Letting people know how you think and feel
- Being clear on the outcomes you want in meetings

Professional Success from Personal Indicators

Indicators are personal. Even so, the resulting impact on leaders' work is immediate and visible. Using such indicators results in leaders

- Who are easily understood.
- With improved relationships.
- Who are more focused on inspiring outcomes.

Others observe this. They see leaders attentive and engaged with their peers and staff. They see new approaches. They see better results. Engagement scores improve.

Leaders with presence have a much stronger sense of themselves and their impact. They function better in their teams. The whole agenda shifts, as does what they talk about. These leaders are more likely to have conversations they want to have, with people they want to have them with. They stop using formulaic responses, cut out habitual unhelpful responses, and run great meetings. They are personable and purposeful.

The two main shifts leaders with presence make are:

1. In addition to content expertise, they contribute to organizational direction. They share their views on how well something will work and how to successfully implement a new direction, service, or product.
2. They share their observations and preferences. This means they challenge the status quo and put the "elephants in the room" onto the agenda. They put these things on the leadership agenda expecting that bosses and peers engage.

Be it diversity, community engagement, clarifying understanding, or assessing the real impact of programs, leaders with presence shape the agenda with observable results.

Big Benefits Result from Behavioral Learning

Effective communication and relationship-building skills will never emerge from studying in isolation. It's the wrong strategy. What works is ensuring relationships and communication are interdependent. They go together. It is impossible to learn to truly engage with people from books or online courses.

As a young professional, I had the pleasure of a breakfast meeting with Charles Handy, the revolutionary management philosopher who set up the London Business School. I asked him what had been his most helpful leadership development experience. He replied, "The encounter groups of the 1960s." That our lives and interactions are our leadership material is nothing new. Your own life and current relationships contain all the leadership material you need to become effective. You might need assistance in accessing this material to use it wisely to engage and inspire individuals and groups.

Leaders often encounter unprecedented situations; contexts change, key drivers shift, team cultures need to be refreshed, crises occur, and new responses are required. Developing relationships and communication capacities requires leaders to be open to ongoing learning.

In organizations, relationships and communication are everyone's business. The effects of poor relationships and poor communication radiate across the business in the informal conversations of frustrated leaders and staff.

Engaging staff is the number-one concern of leaders—as well it should be. As Amy Adkins of Gallup reported, 35 percent of U.S. managers were engaged in their jobs. She goes on to say, "Managers have the greatest impact on employee engagement, so this finding is very worrisome. This study also reported fifty-one percent are not engaged and fourteen percent are actively disengaged."[2]

Gallup estimates the "not engaged" group costs the U.S. $77 billion–$96 billion annually. When the "actively disengaged" groups are factored in, those figures jump to $319 billion–$398 billion. There is something seriously wrong in our organizations. How can staff engage with clients when leaders don't engage with their staff? Leaders' executive presence is an imperative for the bottom line of any organization. Measuring employee engagement is one valuable metric.

---

[2] Adkins, "Only 35% of U.S. Managers Are Engaged in Their Jobs," *Gallup Business Journal*.

Organization Metrics

Behavioral learning efforts can have enormous value to organizations. Having a strong executive presence not only helps you complete what is on the agenda, it helps you shift it to a higher place. The goals for the organization grow and expand, and the leader's clarity and confidence inspires others to go to new places. These leaders have greater faith in themselves and can quickly respond to critical threats. People they relate to feel heard and understood. Leaders with presence help organizations achieve unexpected results and engender flexibility, vitality, and originality.

CASE STUDY: JANET

Vice President Janet was stressed. With eighteen direct reports, she was overwhelmed with meetings she didn't want to be in. She was concerned she was not gaining traction with critical strategic projects. Everyone seemed to want a piece of her, and her diary was full to overflowing. When I asked what her agenda was in meetings, she looked at me. "I don't even want to have them," she retorted. I said, "What meetings do *you* want to have?" She and I discussed options.

Janet stopped her fortnightly hour-long performance discussions with each of her eleven direct reports. She instituted a ten-minute daily stand-up for business and fifteen-minute-maximum meetings for anyone who wanted to consult her. Her direct reports were asked to identify what they wanted from Janet at the beginning of each meeting, whether it was giving an update, Janet being a sounding board, making a decision, or consulting on a direction. Each of her managers was asked to send a brief weekly email listing results and actions taken on risk.

Immediately her diary freed up, and Janet relaxed. She and her staff were well informed. She shifted her focus to strategic matters that had previously been swamped by day-to-day business. Janet's challenge was to break free from what she was supposed to conform to, to what worked. Growing up in the Pacific within a group of thirty cousins, going against adults' expectations was frowned upon. Janet had transferred that expectation to her current situation, and of course it didn't work for her, her staff, or the organization.

Jeff Snipes and Jami York found that while U.S. organizations spent $9 billion a year on formal leadership development programs,

- Less than half (40 percent) have metrics in place to evaluate the overall effectiveness of their leadership development practices.
- Only 55 percent monitor objectives on an ongoing basis.[3]

Behnam Tabrizi found "nearly 75 percent of cross-functional teams are dysfunctional. They fail on at least three of five criteria: 1) meeting a planned budget; 2) staying on schedule; 3) adhering to specifications; 4) meeting customer expectations; and/or 5) maintaining alignment with the company's corporate goals."[4]

Tabrizi identified the five causes of dysfunction:

1. Lack of a systemic approach
2. Unclear governance
3. Lack of accountability
4. Goals that lack specificity
5. Organizations' failure to prioritize the success of cross-functional projects.

Each of these indicates leadership gaps, and each can be rapidly addressed by leaders' accepting and enacting their mandate.

Why has measuring the impact of leaders' development been avoided? What metrics are helpful and to whom? What are essential metrics for organizations success? This is where the rubber hits the road. Individual and organizational metrics shift rapidly as C-suite focus changes. How

---

[3] Snipes and York, "Leadership Development Practices of Top-Performing Organizations."

[4] Tabrizi, Behnam, "Collaboration." *Harvard Business Review*.

do organizations balance leadership development's ROI with the bottom line? Here are some relevant metrics:

- Eliminate time-wasting meetings.
- Work through others and delivers results.
- Communicate simply, clearly, and often.
- Maintain positive relationships when the going gets tough.
- Lead with clear vision, direction, and expectations.
- Improve team or organization engagement scores.
- Maintain positive stakeholder relationships.
- Reduce cost of recruitment and retention.

Significant value is derived from each of these metrics; the key is deciding which to use. The best ones are relevant to the context, don't require expensive and time-consuming research, and are meaningful to both individual leaders and anyone interested in value for money. Responding to the question "What do C-suite leaders want from their investment in leadership development?" will gain a lot. Anecdotal evidence brings life to numbers—stories from participants, observations by leaders, and accounts from staff of their experience.

Deciding Who You Want to Involve in Your Development

It is best to continue this practice for several months after any development program. Leaders' default behaviors typically arise from earlier experiences of isolation. This has implications for measuring success. It is important to ensure any assessments of progress do not replicate earlier experiences of isolation. This can be mitigated by ensuring leaders choose three or four people they want to be involved in their development to help assess their progress. I ask my clients to do this and they regularly identify a peer, one or two people more senior to them, and sometimes a boss or staff member. I suggest they let these people know what they want to develop and invite them to share their observations three or four months after any development program.

This allows respondents to

- Be observant of the leader.
- Give the leader time to implement their learning.
- Reflect on whatever new approaches they notice.
- Deliver thoughtful and contextually grounded feedback.

Leaders then invite responses to the questions (1) "What new things have you noticed in my approach?" and (2) "What is your 'take' on progress I have made toward achieving my outcomes?" Leaders can choose to have these conversations either individually or with the respondents as a group. This process strengthens working relationships between the leader and their chosen respondents.

The New Zealand public sector implemented *career boards* for senior leaders, in which three chief executives meet and discuss a leader's development with them. Their purpose is to provide oversight, guidance, and direction. This example of active interest in leaders' development by respected others inspires most people to step up. This is the very thing that was most often missing in significant moments in earlier life.

Practice Session 7.1

Review your responses from the interpersonal perceptions profile of chapter 6.

Identify three outcomes you want for greater executive presence.

1. _____

2. _____

3. _____

Identify three success indicators. What would you be doing? What would others see you do to achieve the outcomes you want? What response would you want from others?

1. _____
2. _____
3. _____

How would you know if you were successful in achieving your outcomes? What would the results be?

1. _____
2. _____
3. _____

Summary

- With executive presence, you need signs to know you have reached the outcomes you want.
- Identifying outcomes for executive presence means you already have a vision for yourself beyond what exists now.
- When you set outcomes, the things that have held you back or tripped you up are no longer in the front of your mind.
- Behavior change takes time.
- Leaders with presence engage and develop relationships with aggrieved parties to move things forward.
- Being accountable and reporting results is an age-old mechanism that works.
- Leaders with presence are more likely to have conversations they really want to have, with people they want to have them with.
- When leaders experience the desired response with their new approaches, their delight and sense of achievement reinforces the new behavior.

- Ensure that assessment methods do not replicate earlier experiences of isolation.
- The interest of respected figures in one's leadership development inspires most people to step up.

Chapter 8

A Leopard Can Change Its Spots

CHANGING BEHAVIOR IS POSSIBLE even if you feel completely stressed, frustrated, or helpless in your work. This chapter gives clues, practical concepts, and a language for describing behavior that enables fresh approaches to familiar situations.

How often are you caught in unhelpful behavioral patterns? How much do your fears and anxieties hold you back? Threaded throughout this chapter are touchstones that can be used in working with leaders' development.

My work as a leadership coach is inspired by one long-held vision: to see leaders approaching difficult situations with freshness and vitality. Leaders learn that lacking a particular ability is not a life sentence but rather a challenge to embrace. They learn they have inner resources and the capacity to use them. They learn to reach out to others. I envision a world where leaders do not believe they are on their own, but see themselves as an integral part of a creative group of professionals.

Many of us have had life experiences where hurts, resentments, frustrations, love, and joy were not fully or adequately expressed at the time. Aspects of our genuine self, that central creative capacity enabling us to learn and create, are burned and withered by certain early life experiences. We develop coping strategies that isolate us from others. Bruised and hurt, we want to hide and refrain from expressing ourselves fully and freely, or we interact in ways that bruise and hurt others. We can lose heart or be defensive in the face of criticism, negativity, or the roadblocks that litter our way. We forget we are creative beings with many capacities. However, if we take time to reflect and expand our vision for ourselves, we reconnect with our creative self. We can develop new responses to everyday encounters while relating to those around us. We can shift from a state of anxious impotence to knowing how we can be of service.

Primary learning methods help leaders shift from an overly intellectual approach to reading people, emotions, and relationships. They shift from remembering facts to reading facial and body movements. They listen to people. They tune into and trust their intuition and perceptions of what is happening. They learn to purposefully connect with bosses, peers, and staff. They access and share their vision while helping people to connect with ideas and one another.

Changing Behavior Is Possible

Astonishingly, minor shifts in behavior have major positive impacts. These behavior changes are associated with complex psychological and emotional shifts.

Three key actions help make you make these shifts:

- Realizing you are not alone and that others share your experience.
- Understanding and accepting the origin of your default behaviors.
- Assessing the relevance of the behavior from then to now.

Traditional feedback misses the mark because recipients rarely understand what is being said to them. Leaders with presence do not present dry analyses of behavior; rather, they are skilled at sharing astute descriptions.

CASE STUDY: MARK

I'm meeting with Mark and his manager, Neil. I ask, What is the area you want Mark to develop? Neil talks with Mark. "You know this stuff backwards; you address poor performance. You are a trusted adviser to me and SLT. Here are things I want you to work on. When you are challenged you are too polite. Your voice wavers. In these moments you lose your confidence.""What does he do?" I ask. "His voice wavers—I can hear him sucking his breath in. "Mark relaxes and laughs. Neil continues, "You focus on risks rather than daring to share your insight on possibilities." Slightly embarrassed, Mark recognizes his behavior. Immediately Mark has something practical to work on, as Neil's observations are immediately helpful. Neil is a master detective who has spotted Mark's default behavior. Mark's development plan with me could then take shape.

Metaphors Matter

Of course, leaders have a wide range of progressive behaviors for use in a variety of group environments and situations. They use their judgment in what works where. What we are considering here are behaviors related to a leader's specific development goals. These behaviors are personalized and context related and appear in specific situations or relationships.

Leaders use metaphors to stimulate the imagination in transcribing the unknown to the known. Metaphors simply describe complex experiences: "I have been stabbed in the back," "This is a steep learning curve," and "It's clean sailing from here." With primary learning, people associate readily at the "feeling level"—something makes sense.

Labels (defensive, aggressive, calm) are judgmental and overly restrictive, but describing behavior in colorful metaphors can lead to new possibilities. Metaphoric descriptions that accurately reflect the impact of the behavior will create a vivid picture of the issue at hand.

Behavioral metaphors are lively descriptions that include thinking, feeling, and action components.[1,2] This is best done with several adjectives and a noun. Of course, any assessment is partial. If clients are interested, I share my observations, and we refine the metaphors together.

---

[1] Lynette Clayton, "The Use of the Cultural Atom."
[2] Max Clayton, "The Preparation and Writing of a Social and Cultural Atom Paper."

Horney identifies three subsets of overdeveloped default behaviors: moving toward people, moving away from people, and moving against people. Below are a few typical behaviors of leaders within these three categories.

I have applied Clayton and Clayton's approaches in working with leaders and use two of Horney's three original behavioral categories, default (coping) and progressive.[3] I don't work with fragmenting behaviors in business settings. Fragmenting behaviors actively sabotage relationships and reciprocity. Typical examples are the *relentless bully*, the *acerbic persistent critic*, and the *furious accuser*. For the most part, leaders are already high functioning; I see my work with them as fine-tuning. Leadership development is not about personality makeovers; it is about expanding one's capacity to relate well with others and to function effectively in stressful situations.

We all have default behaviors. Identifying four or five overdeveloped behaviors in a development context is helpful for leaders, as is identifying up to five emerging progressive behaviors. These are usually embryonic, but they are evident. While emerging behaviors are observable, leaders have to consciously practice them until they can be accessed by choice. (see figure 8.5.)

Metaphor	Thinking	Feeling	Action
The friendly, empathetic host	I'm friendly so that people will like me. Others are more important than me.	Anxiety	Helping others
The persistently self-deprecating joker	I'll get in first so no one can get me. If I make people laugh, they will like me.	Anxiety	Hide the real self and display the funny self

FIGURE 8.1   Typical "Moving Toward" Default Behaviors

---

[3] Horney, *Our Inner Conflicts.*

Metaphor	Thinking	Feeling	Action
The verbose, dedicated historian	I need to take charge here and talk about what has happened.	Anxiety	Hide in a flurry of words
The silently perceptive critical analyst	I need to hide and watch until I can work out what is happening. Don't feel or say anything.	Anxiety	Observe and analyze

FIGURE 8.2   Typical "Moving Away" Default Behaviors

Metaphor	Thinking	Feeling	Action
The competitive, acerbic street fighter	Blunt is best. Fight for your life. I know the truth.	Anger and invisibility	Argue, tell it like it is, or cut people out
The brusque, voluble high court judge	I say it like it is. My idea is the best one, and I know what's right.	Frustration	I lay down the law

FIGURE 8.3   Typical "Moving Against" Default Behaviors

Metaphor	Thinking	Feeling	Action
The personable, insightful context setter and navigator	I see a way forward.	Wise and insightful	Takes an overview, reads the terrain, and proposes a direction
The collegial, vulnerable storyteller	I want to connect.	Open	Share a personal story

FIGURE 8.4   Typical Progressive Roles

| Fragmenting | | Default | | | Progressive | |
Diminishing	Unchanged	Moving toward people	Moving away from people	Moving against people	Well developed	Emerging
X	X	Houdini in disguise	The hard-working under-the-radar lost boy The worried watchful silent analyst The forthright long-winded futurist	The determined impatient action man	Leaders have many well-developed progressive behaviors. Using wise judgment, they activate these in a variety of settings; otherwise they wouldn't be undertaking the work they are doing.	The personable appreciative navigator The collegial vivid storyteller The perceptive terrain reader and inviter of action The encouraging companionable colleague The inclusive affirming expectation and direction setter

FIGURE 8.5   A Tailored Assessment Looks Like This

These are my observations of a leader's interactions in a group setting as they moved away from their goals (overdeveloped default behaviors) and when they moved toward their goals (emerging progressive behaviors).

Both default and progressive behaviors operate as if they were in a 3-D cluster—different behaviors coming to the fore in response to different situations. The main distinction between default and progressive behaviors is that each progressive role is relational. The leader's response to this assessment would guide my work with them over the next months.

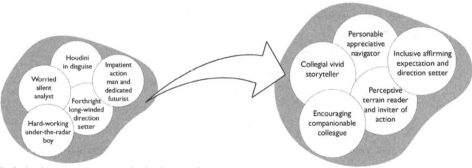

Default cluster moves into the background

Progressive cluster moves into the foreground

FIGURE 8.6 The Clusters of Progressive Behaviors Come to the Foreground

More Insights with Chris

Chris is personable, bright, and articulate. Leading a team of specialists within the production sector, Chris emanates warmth and charm. In our group sessions, he is readily chosen as a confidant and described as approachable or looking like a leader. During our work together, peers consistently invite him to play the challenging executive in their live scenarios. He takes up these roles with vitality and acutely replicates the ascribed characteristics, ensuring the scene is an accurate reflection of his colleagues' scenarios.

Over the three group sessions, several behavioral themes become apparent. I notice that in stressful settings, Chris has overdeveloped default behaviors in each subset: moving toward, moving away, and moving against. My first guess is that bosses and peers might perceive him as an ambivalent leader, sometimes hot and on the mark and sometimes cold. My second guess is that Chris would feel the same thing himself, and that he would be more likely to respond when invited rather than initiate.

None of my assessment is of value to Chris unless he invites me to comment. I may never discover why Chris has these behaviors, but that is not the point. How well does this assessment mirror Chris' behavior as he knows himself? It turns out when we discuss this together that my observations were accurate.

Chris and I continued our work in one-on-one meetings. In response to my assessment, he let me know he was frightened most of the time. I was shocked at first but quickly accepted it as truth. The dissonance among his default behaviors now made sense. One ensuing conversation went as follows:

Diana: Where is *fear* in relation to you?
           (Here, Diana is working as a sociometrist.)

Chris: Right beside me.
           (Diana reflects upon the fact that clients always know precisely where someone stands in relation to them. She places a chair beside Chris.)

Diana: Here he is.
           (Chris looks askance. Instinctively, he puts his arm around *fear*.)

Diana: Hold on tight. Don't let him go.
           (Chris looks at Diana questioningly.)

Diana: Hiding *fear* and pretending he doesn't exist won't work. Accept your *fear*. Hold your *fear* close to you. Take *fear* with you. Think of *fear* as you did when you were young. So there's you now, and there's the frightened you from earlier. For some reason, the frightened you was ignored."
           (Chris lets this experience sink in. The session exercise concludes. Chris heads off to his next meeting.)

---

*Little of the content in coaching leaders makes
logical sense. Predefined techniques don't work,
and the coach works without preconceived ideas or
a plan.*

The four principles operating here are that 1) every interaction with the leader is in the here and now; 2) an object can represent an abstract idea or experience; 3) work is focused on assisting the client move toward their outcomes; and 4) the coach trusts the client's process and the results of their work.

A few days later, I received a text from Chris. "Fear is a funny fellow. He's beside me all the time. I'm calling him IT" (from Stephen King's novel). My silent assessment is that Chris' relationship with his genuine self is strengthening. I don't respond to Chris' update.

CASE STUDY: CHRIS

Six months later I interviewed Chris. I asked him to describe his experience of our work together. He recalled the first group session in the Executive Presence program. Chris said, "Early on, I felt cold and nervous. I was trying to assess all the other people that were there. What I liked was that we immediately began working together and breaking down some of those barriers. A lot of ego stuff gets going when you first get together in a group. We are all making judgments and assessments of one another. *Why are all of you here? Some of you don't even look like leaders.* Suddenly I was asking myself, How will I manage myself in this meeting when there's someone else I know here? How do we negotiate this experience? I'm a director; he's a L4 manager. Mixed in on top of that was the feeling of insecurity. The environment was unfamiliar. I was with people I didn't really know, I realized I would have to be quite open with these people. The fear came in.

"The fear came in," I said. I had the sense that the fear was familiar.

Chris continued, "For me, success has always been driven from the fear of failure. I had a strong self-critic. Every environment I enter, whether I'm with my leadership team, or with SLT, or the public, I've been able to hide fear quite well. I've been compensating. I can give an air of confidence. The external me is seen to have confidence, but internally I lack confidence. There's a scared boy there. The challenge was that in the short term I could be confident. Over time, people got to know me, and the protective barriers fell down. The real me became present and I dropped from being a leader to being a follower. I was less able to get my opinion across. I was less able to be firm in my opinion. I was more in a collaborative or consensus mode rather than being the leader."

"Where did the fear come from?" I asked in the knowledge Chris had strong self-insight.

"When I was four years old, I was sent to a private boarding school. I was away from my family and felt terrified. Early on in school I didn't do so well. I got better when I moved from English subjects to science and math. But I had a lot of fear of failing exams. The school was a traditional "old English" school. We were strapped if we didn't do things right. All that sort of thing. I feared the hierarchy. I was scared of doing things wrong. My dad had a fiery temper. He'd chase me down the street with a cricket bat if I'd been naughty. So fear became familiar. There was a lot of fear and anxiety around home and at school.

Then I was set adrift in private practice. That reminded me how I'd felt when I first went to school. That was a familiar feeling—of being set adrift and my fear of failure.

I'd worked with coaches before and had worked with mindfulness. I was aware fear had been driving me. My coaches had said to me, "*You can't tame something unless you can get hold of it.*" Fear was a state of feeling and I didn't know how to get hold of a feeling.

In our work together, I was able to grasp my "frightened me" and hold on. What was liberating was that someone (me) cared enough to hold that frightened person. I literally put my arm around my fear and held on.

I started to explore that with my leadership team and during presentations. As soon as the fear started to come up, I could sit there and watch the fear coming out of me. When I felt that, I don't want to be in this room; I'd like to leave, I would stay still and see my fear wanting to walk out of the room. Then I'd visualize myself grabbing it, pulling it back, and saying, "It's OK. I'm here to help you." That released the tension and the pain.

Diana: "Fear had a caring companion."

Chris continues, "I can't come across authentic when there is fear." So now I do presentations to my staff on being customer-centric. I am authentic. I'm more confident and feel free. I'm no longer looking at the audience wondering what they are thinking about me. I'm concentrating on delivering the message and how I am delivering the message rather than wondering how I am being perceived."

"I recognize my fear as 'someone' who comes out from time to time. Someone who wants to run. I can live with that. I'm now more relaxed in my role and with my staff. There's less stress at work. A weight has lifted from my shoulders."

"I now have the ability to see fear for what it is. I sleep better. Rather than listen to my fears at night, I just say, I'll deal with that tomorrow."

"I put things into perspective. It's enabled me to do things I would have turned down before and to lead the company's national road show. I can concentrate on what I want to deliver to the audience. Fear isn't overwhelming anymore; I know where it belongs."

Chris has a new dilemma. His success was driven by fear of failure. Now that has gone, he is looking around for what he really wants to do. He doesn't yet know.

Circuit Breakers

Leaders' typical responses to draft assessments (e.g. figure 8.5) include:

- I really like all my characters.
- I recognize myself.
- I notice when I am falling back into these defaults.

- This is like a map: I know when I am over here and I know when I'm here.

They might respond with, "Tell me how this one works. I don't relate to this." When I hear this, I know I have made a mistake and delete it from the assessment.

The assessment acts as a mirror as the leader's emotional experience is *doubled*. Doubling occurs when someone or something reflects aloud, or internally a *felt experience*.

When there are finely tuned relationships between coach and client and/or among peers, doubling is possible. The double gives voice to unexpressed "felt" experiences. "You've had a shock," "You feel misunderstood by us," or "You have been working hard, and no one has noticed." The double is nonjudgmental. Effective doubles follow with, "Is that right?" When leaders in distress are accurately doubled, they no longer feel isolated. A bridge has been built so they can make sense of their experience. There is a psychoemotional forward movement as value clashes are revealed and their self-acceptance expands. New insights are possible. However, if the relationship between the double and the leader is not positive, the double will be rejected.

Doubling is key to the formation of a child's early identity and healthy development. The caregiver doubles the baby. Therapists might double their clients to reflect their appreciation of a client's experience. Doubling communicates an appreciation and understanding of what the "other" is experiencing. This involves more than just empathy.

When leaders overlook colleagues' and employees' *felt experience*, they ignore the most useful tool they have for implementing change. When leaders don't care, it confirms and reinforces the stereotype of the ruthless, money-driven leader.

Leaders fall into traps when they misread their finely tuned relationships. They might make an analysis of another's faults and become critical and judgmental to the point of obsession. They can't see anything positive. The person can't do anything right. The leader uses techniques like the feedback sandwich but nothing rings true to the recipient. Doubling is neither possible nor advisable in settings where your relationship is negative. If you try to double, you will be rejected even if you are accurate.

With sensitive timing and the help of a *trusted, purposeful companion or coach*, leaders feel seen, accepted, and expanded. Long-held feelings and uncertainties finally make sense.

Like any mirror, the behavioral assessment is a snapshot of a moment in time; any value in retaining this assessment solely belongs to its leader. When an assessment of a leader is accurate, self-knowledge is affirmed and self-acceptance increases. Their concept of themselves expands. There are no value judgments in the metaphors. The experience of receiving an accurate mirror and double, including both positive and not positive elements, is affirmative and real. Recipients begin to unconsciously implement their progressive roles, and their new behaviors are reinforced by the positive responses they get. All they have now is the challenge of practicing and strengthening those behaviors. The only way is through practice, practice, practice.

What works here is the positive interactive loop that is generated. The leader recognizes the old situation, knows where it comes from, has a moment of choice, chooses a new approach, sets indicators to track, and receives positive responses from others. They experience success, and the behavior is reinforced.

When metaphors are inaccurate, it leads to a loss of vitality. Leaders might ask, "What did I see? How does that work?" When I hear these questions, I know my assessment has generated doubt rather than vitality, and I change course.

No Size Fits All

It is essential for leadership development to be personalized. There are four magic bullets:

1. The leader wants to be inspiring in interpersonal and group connections.

2. The leader has or develops trusting relationships with bosses, colleagues, or their leadership coach.

3. The leader is willing to learn through experience, reflection, insight, and action.

4. The leader gently and firmly works toward the development outcomes they seek.

The four magic bullets for coaches:

1. The coach develops trusted relationships rapidly.

2. The coach is guided completely by their client's purpose and outcomes.

3. The coach stays in collaborative relationships.

4. The coach has client interactions based on respect.

FIGURE 8.7 The Learning Process

Each leader's learning process is different. Behavior change is complex and can take time. Like Chris, some experience significant shifts in behavior over several months, while others achieve their outcomes in the first meeting. Some might take a year to achieve the outcomes they want.

The key thing is to set observable metrics so leaders and invited others can track their progress.

Being seen, understood, and accepted is a powerful experience for anyone. Some leaders consciously work with originating events over time. It is enough for others to know that there is a foundation for their default behavior; they can accept it and move forward. The coach's function is to personalize their learning and help generate options for responding in the future.

Just Whose Business Is This?

It is the leader's business to:

- Identify overdeveloped default behaviors, or be aware when someone you trust has done so for you.
- Set development outcomes for specific situations and with specific groups.
- Accept the likely origin of the overdeveloped default behavior.
- Thoughtfully cut the link between then and now.
- Be open to new responses more aligned with your values and current context.

Other than the setting of development outcomes, each step is a private and personal process. Whether you share any of this is your personal decision. Make this decision wisely.

This approach poses a dilemma for bosses and organizations that want massive systems for developing leaders. None of this information belongs to the organization other than perhaps the outcomes being set and how overall success is measured. Some leaders I know share their behavioral assessment with trusted bosses. Mostly this remains private between myself and the person I am working with. I encourage leaders to have a conversation with specified others four months after our work together, starting with the question "What changes have you noticed in how I am responding?" Frequently I am involved in those conversations.

Documenting any personal information with these methods is wrong. Any assessment is powerful, but it serves its purpose in the moment.

Integrating Thinking, Feeling, and Action

What causes a person to shift from overdeveloped default behaviors to progressive behaviors? In essence, what factors causes a person to move from isolation to connecting with others?

1. Knowing others share your experience of anxiety, lack of confidence, or low self-esteem
2. Accepting the experience of connecting with others, can be simultaneously powerful, painful, and positive:
    a. Powerful in that the leader realizes they are alive
    b. Painful due to the loss of the transference that once overlaid interactions
    c. Positive through the integration of thinking, feeling, and action
3. Wanting greater competency and leadership effectiveness
4. Enabling social intelligence

When leaders integrate thinking, feeling, and action, they create psychological and emotional relief both in themselves and others.

Practice Session 8.1

1. Write down what you do in response to a specific person or event, including
    - Your thinking.
    - Your feelings.

- Your actions. (Do you go silent, explain, walk away, argue, hide, or freeze?)

2. Describe your behavior in response to this specific situation and think of a metaphor for yourself. Use two vivid adjectives for the thinking and feeling components of your behavior, followed by a noun.

3. Draw two circles, one representing the original event and one representing your current response. Now draw a line between the two events. Write down five to ten of your successes, achievements, or new capacities along the line in between.

4. Make a new drawing showing the new relationship you *want* to have between the two events.

5. Generate three options of how you could respond in your current situation.

Summary

- Realize that not having a particular ability is not a life sentence; it is a challenge to embrace.
- Primary learning methods help you shift from intellectualizing to reading people, emotions, and relationships.
- Minor shifts in behavior have major positive impacts.
- Doubling builds a bridge so people can make sense of their experience.
- When you reflect colleagues and employees' *felt experience*, you have a key to implementing change and taking people with you.
- Being seen, understood, and accepted is a powerful experience for anyone.

Chapter 9

Final Touches:
The Language of Leadership

A s a leader, the most immediate asset you have is your language. Choosing your words wisely directly impacts your influence and success. This chapter outlines the nature of communication and provides guidelines on how to make your leadership language clear and purposeful.

Grammar didn't interest me at school because I could see no use for it. But as I learned rudimentary French, Italian, and Te Reo (Maori), I began to see the purpose of grammar, and now it fascinates me. The value of accurate grammar is nowhere more evident than when I am coaching leaders. I can hear when leaders lose the vitality in their interactions and see the positive impact when they speak directly to listeners. I see the dull impact of leaders when they talk *about* people rather than [to] them. The important grammatical terms you will encounter here are pronouns, verbs, singular and plural forms, and active and passive voice.

Whether through e-mail, conversation, or uplifting speech, your language communicates your vision, inspires those around you, and helps you convey what is important. The words you say and write are the central mechanism that attracts others, clarifies tasks, and generates excitement.

How can you make your leadership language clear and purposeful? We'll start by looking at what communication actually is, and how it comprises more than just the obvious content. Then, we'll examine three words—"I," "you," and "we"—to powerfully convey your presence. With these three words, you can produce

- Collaboration and engagement
- Accountability
- Differentiation.

Choosing your language wisely directly impacts your influence and success.

The Two Messages

As leaders, one of our main jobs is to humanize the workplace such that the staff is inspired to do their best work. But language can be tricky.

In the early 1960s, UCLA's Albert Mehrabian conducted research that remains relevant to leaders everywhere.[1] He found that every act of communication has two messages: a content message and a relationship message. The content message is the meat of what you want to say: "I want us to increase sales by 10 percent this quarter," "We will shift our model for making investment decisions," or, "The project deadline is in exactly ten days."

Your content message enables you to:

- Make requests.
- Give facts.
- Share vision.
- Provide direction.
- Impart information.
- Delegate tasks.
- Outline context and expectations.

---

[1] Mehrabian, *Silent Messages.*

The second is the relationship message. It conveys both how you feel and your attitude toward the receivers. Your relationship message is conveyed through words, tone, body language, and facial expressions.

Mehrabian broke down how a speaker's attitudes and feelings directly influence others as follows:

- 7 percent by their choice of words
- 38 percent by the tone of their voice
- 55 percent by their facial expressions

Mehrabian's research has at least two implications. The first is that every time you communicate, attending to both messages is essential. How you speak will make people feel either included and valued or excluded and rejected. Powerful stuff.

Each Word Is Important

The second implication is that while only 7 percent of the relationship message is contained in spoken words, each word is important.

In e-mail, 100 percent of meaning is "conveyed through the choice of words and how they are written: syntax, punctuation, letter case, the length of your sentences and how you [open and close] the email."[2] This is especially important given that the number of sent and received daily business e-mails is expected to grow to 132.1 billion by 2017.[3] E-mail has several quirks that interpersonal communication doesn't. E-mail enables us to transact business without having a personal relationship with people. A familiarity is assumed in e-mail that may not be present in person. While e-mail protocols help enormously, offending recipients is easy. Attending to your tone in e-mails wins people or loses them.

---

[2] Swink, "Don't Type at Me Like That! Email and Emotions. Emails have feelings too." *Psychology Today.* 2013
[3] Radicati and Levenstein, Email Statistics Report, 2013–2017.

So What Really Matters?

Many leaders communicate as if relationship messages are irrelevant to serious work. But ignoring the relationship message is the fastest way to alienate people. When leaders do so, they're assuming they know what's best and find excuses for lacking empathy. The recipients, though, will react and draw away from these leaders because they want their contributions to count. Also, leaders who assume they are right have only half the picture; they miss out on engaging the very people they rely on to make things work.

Earlier leadership paradigms failed because no attention was paid to the relationship message. Unless there is an emergency, a relationship of legal authority (such as warden to inmate), or a specific skill or technique is being taught (surgery or fixing a computer glitch), ordering people to act causes resentment. People want to be treated as intelligent and worthwhile. They want to know that their lives and work are valued.

The Communication Paradigm Is Changing

Only a few decades ago, communication was much different than it is today. International phone calls were expensive, traveling long distances was prohibitive, and a letter would take nearly a week to reach its final destination.

Now the world is a global village. International travel is speedy and inexpensive. Cell phones are the size of playing cards. E-mail and texts dominate interpersonal communication, and newspapers are electronic. I can talk with international colleagues for an hour on my cell phone, and it costs me only $2.

New Approaches Are Required

Whether in writing or speaking, leaders cannot ignore the context in which their words are interpreted. For the same reason that command

and control paradigms are less effective than ones of influence and collaboration, a purely logical and rational approach to using language is less than ideal.

Your language as a leader reflects:

- How you collaborate and engage
- How you demonstrate your accountability
- Your capacities for positive mutual tele
- How well you read responses from individuals and groups
- How you convey your authority through your vision and direction

Be conscious of how you regard the receiver as you tailor your message. No longer can leaders consider communication as "information out, information in." Do not hide behind your technical expertise or formally appointed role. As a leader with presence, you are responsible for creating a culture of engagement and participation, and communication is the central tool for shaping relationships with those around you. Ignore the relationship message at your peril. When people feel disregarded and undermined, they are likely to return the favor.

Specificity and Tone

The use of specific words makes you either powerful, genuine, and purposeful or bossy, abrupt, and confrontational. Your tone can shift people's perceptions of you and your message, creating either alignment or division among disparate groups.

When aligned with action, language is not just a technique. Your choice of words and style of delivery enable you to enact your role as leader.

Recipients tune into the *relationship* message first, which directly affects how they interpret the *content* of the message. Established working relationships allow for more flexibility in communication. Bosses, peers, and staff are more accepting once they know you have their best interests at heart.

Relationships quickly break down if you forget or overemphasize the relationship message—and especially if you communicate from your default behaviors. Bosses, peers, and staff quickly realize when they are disrespected. Cooperation ceases. Conversations shift from productive work to informal conversations to how people feel about you.

Learning to discern relationship messages is highly beneficial even in the short term. People recognize when you use techniques. A leader might use the "right" words, but unless their emotional tone is genuine, the intended message will not be received.

What helps is aligning your actions and your words.

Why People Can't Hear You

Calling someone out in a critical, loud, or angry tone conveys a lack of respect. Anyone receiving this kind of message is likely to feel personally attacked. They are unlikely even to fully receive your content message, let alone accept it with goodwill or apply their best efforts. As relationships deteriorate, people will simply comply and do little more. They are likely to emotionally "move away" from you and become distrustful and highly stressed.

A sought-after public sector technology disrupter tells me she "physically recoils" when leaders communicate with her in a harsh tone or without a personal relationship message.

Three Simple Words Pack Power

If you want to have positive personal relationships, three words in particular are incredibly powerful. If you use them wisely, these words—"I," "you," and "we"—will be your greatest allies. Let's talk about how they are both used and misused.

These "power words" give you language for

- Creating unity, engagement, and collaboration.
- Differentiating yourself from peers.
- Engaging with others.
- Demonstrating accountability.
- Providing vision and direction.

If you misuse these three words, you are in big trouble. Others will see you as

- Faceless.
- Self-centered.
- Irrelevant.
- Uninspiring.
- Impersonal.
- Unaccountable.

As leader, you have a choice. You can either create connections with your words or cause alienation. You can include or exclude, talk directly to people or about them. You can produce vitality and inspiration or leave others cold.

> *Learning the personal and active language of leadership—the effective use of "I," "you," and "we"—enhances your capacity to inspire others and will give your presence a significant boost.*

The Language of Collaboration and Engagement—"You" and "We"

Learning the language of engagement can dramatically impact your bottom line. After working with leaders with both high and low team engagements scores, I noticed some distinctive differences in their communication styles.

Leaders with High Engagement Scores	Leaders with Low Engagement Scores
• Clear use of "I," "you," and "we" • Succinct • Shares expectations and direction • I want you to . . . (inspiration) • Results oriented • Future oriented	• Woolly use of "I," "you," and "we" • Verbose • Describes or overexplains context • I need you to . . . (obligation) • Performance oriented • Problem focused

FIGURE 9.1 Language for Engagement

Every group is made up of people with disparate opinions, ideas, and experiences. Your role as leader is to create unity of purpose by providing direction. How on earth do you do that? One way is with language—after clearly expressing your goals and expectations, people can choose how to respond and contribute. Be conscious of when to include everyone and when to differentiate subgroups. Help people to participate.

Talking to People or about Them

In everyday language, "we" is a pronoun used by speakers to include themselves and one or more others. Leaders can use "we" to promote collaboration and a sense of inclusion in peer groups and with their own team.

How many times have you listened to a leader talking *about* their team rather than *to* them?

Michael kicks off his weekly team meeting. "The team has done a great job." Team members look back blankly. I was confused. Is Michael talking to his team? About his team? Or about another team?

This is often the moment when the emotional tone of the group shifts from anticipation to disappointment, and a crucial opportunity for engagement is lost. Michael distances himself from his team by his language. His default behavior is evident as he adopts the role of the *anxious, faceless appreciator*, fearful of the intimacy that active language creates. I despair when leaders want to engage with their staff yet use language that actively keeps them at a distance. Ironically, leaders who want staff to engage with customers are often themselves unwilling to engage with their staff.

Understanding what people want and how they feel as you communicate the outcomes you want is another key to executive presence.

Other possessive pronouns reflect ownership and collaboration: "ours" and "us." Possessive pronouns with the potential to create divisions in groups are "them," "theirs," "yours." Use these words carefully.

CASE STUDY: MICHAEL

After some coaching and reflection, Michael took a different approach to his opening remarks to the team: "You have all done a great job. You have grappled with the roadblocks and you found ways through. You have shown your determination and steadiness in the face of disappointment. You have held on to the things all of us value as a team. And you have produced this result. I am delighted in your capacities to work together and help one another when the going got tough."

The group has no doubt Michael is talking to them. Each person hears the leader's appreciation and acknowledgment.

When there is a tough problem to face, leaders who use "we" language put themselves right in the thick of it with their team. "We have some tough problems to resolve. We know what the problems are, and we know we are resourceful. Let us make a plan and identify who will do what and what you want from me to make this work."

Leaders who use "you" language have a powerful advantage when speaking to their team, division, or organization. Used as a plural, "you" includes everyone in the group. "You have done a great job." Immediately, listeners respond. The group's emotional tone lifts as people sense that their efforts are recognized. To individualize this acknowledgment, you might say, "We are making progress. Each and every one of you has made a special contribution. Each of you is making a difference." The team understands that their efforts are appreciated, they are making progress, and the leader has referred to everyone involved. Be aware of your use of "I," "we," and "you," and you will possess a powerful language for engaging with others.

CASE STUDY: JANE

Jane is talking with her team. "We have a busy week ahead of us, and we need to focus. Let's look out for one another to ensure that we are delivering results and finding our work satisfying, too." In this example Jane includes herself with her team. The "we" in "We have work to do" is collaborative. Her approach creates a sense of belonging—that we all are in this together.

However, there is a potential downside of using "we." Indiscriminate use enables leaders to hide within a group. Some leaders fall into this trap; in doing so, they avoid accountability.

I continue coaching Jane. She is excited about her work and has been grappling with a complex scenario with many stakeholders. "We are on the verge of making a breakthrough."

I get her excitement, but I also think, Who is we? Who is she including? Is her company on the verge of the breakthrough? Is she referring to the wide range of people on the project across departments? Or is it just her team, or maybe Jane herself? By clarifying, Jane can give her team the opportunity to engage relevantly without making assumptions.

Generate Questions to Include Everyone

Differentiating subgroups along social criteria such as race, gender, senior-ity, or sexual orientation is rarely helpful. Instead, interpersonal connec-tions are best generated by identifying relevant and inclusive subgroups. Avoid passing judgments, stereotyping, and pigeonholing; instead, inclu-sive questions can be used as a gateway for sharing stories, discovering diversity, and enabling further connections.

Leaders can generate inclusion by asking questions everyone relates to. Leadership expert Simon Sinek begins group conversations by asking, "How many of you here have thought about why you do what you do as leaders?" This question is universal and free of cultural bias. Immediately everyone is involved and willing to accept Sinek's invitation to engage.

Inclusive questions allow for people to tap into their thoughtfulness and experience, whether they identify with the main theme or not. People's responses give the questioner important information for refining their content and adapting it to different contexts. Talk directly to people by using "you" and invite them to tap into their experience, particularly their shared experiences.

Inclusive questions include

- What is one of the most difficult situations that you have led as a leader?
- How was conflict managed within your family?
- What has been your best experience of being empowered?
- What is the most important thing for you right now?
- How many of you here have worked on a failed project recently? Anyone not?
- What insights do you have on what helps turn failures around?

Ask questions like these, and people are free to share their personal experiences as they want to. They expand how they present themselves and others rapidly form connections with them.

The Language of Accountability—"I" and "You"

Personal language creates immediacy, bringing everyone into the here and now.

Let's take a closer look at how to use "I" and "you" wisely. Grammatically, "you" is a personal pronoun, and as such, owns the verb which follows. Confusingly, "you" can be either singular (referring to one person) or plural (referring to a group). Oddly, leaders frequently use "you" when in fact they are talking about themselves. This is confusing to listeners, to say the least! How many times have you heard coaches tell leaders, to "use I statements"? You know what I mean!

It is impossible for leaders to demonstrate accountability when they use the ambiguity of language to avoid referring to themselves. By using "you" in this way, the leader hides and avoids responsibility. On the other hand, "I" communicates ownership and accountability.

Consider the phrase "You know we have to do it this way" versus "I want you to do it like this." When leaders use "you" when they mean "I," listeners move away from them and are reluctant to engage. Audiences fear they're being unfairly labeled with some attribute they don't associate with. This is unhelpful.

With "I," the leader takes ownership of their actions, while "and you" creates inclusion. In contrast, "We have work to do" is collaborative but also vague—it is unclear who specifically might be involved.

The ambiguous sentence "We have work to do" is more effective if it is personalized as "You and I have work to do." This is invaluable when you are working in pairs. In this case, "you" is singular and the other person has no doubt you are referring to them. They know precisely who they will be working alongside.

Impersonal and Passive

Passive language is the language of distance—it creates a gap between yourself and your listeners. When leaders use "you" without referring directly to *whom* they are relating, their language is impersonal and passive.

Impersonal language forces listeners to make assumptions. Their minds cast about for interpretations and associations. They are left to decide: does what is being said refer to them or to someone else? The ambiguity that impersonal language creates is a frequent source of misunderstanding among leaders and in meetings.

The Language of Differentiation—Leading Your Peers with "I"

In any group, everyone has a chance to contribute ideas and direction and act in a leadership role. Leading in peer groups requires you to differentiate yourself, and one excellent way to do so is with your language. When embedded within your peer group, you can influence direction with your language while still being perceived as collaborative. By using "we" and "I" thoughtfully, you can stand apart from the crowd.

The ability to collaborate in peer groups is a highly sought-after quality in all organizations. How on earth do you speak up without alienating your colleagues? How do you differentiate your view and remain connected with your boss and peers? Whether you are a leader, an innovator, or a disrupter, knowing how to influence and maintain relationships is essential for advancing your organization's agenda.

The personal pronoun "I" gives you the language of differentiation. By using "I," the speaker unambiguously owns the verb that follows. *I notice, I want, I suggest, I like, I think, I am aware . . .*

CASE STUDY: TALKING OVER EACH OTHER

I am in a meeting where everyone is talking at once. What intervention should I make?

I could cry out, "We are talking over one another, and no one can hear what is being said!" For some in the group, this may be accurate;

however, it is unlikely that everyone is talking at once. Those people will silently disagree and might feel attacked. As the one calling out the behavior, I'm both "hiding" within the group and lumping everyone together.

In the sentence above, "we" is a personal pronoun corresponding to the following verb and suggestive of inclusion and collaboration. This is not the real picture. When you say "We should . . ." or "We need to . . ." in a peer group, perhaps half of the group will agree with you, while the other half will not. By randomly including people, you alienate them and fail to accurately portray the nuanced views in the group.

Here's the ownership version: "I notice we are talking over one another, me included. I don't like it. I want to be in a group where we respect one another. I want to hear what each of you has to say. I propose that each of us . . ." or "How about we . . .?"

In this case study, using "I" differentiates me from my peers. By explicitly owning my assessment of the situation, I provide leadership and my proposal has more weight.

I especially encourage leaders to use "I" when there are a range of views around the table. To invite engagement, make sure to follow up your contribution with a question such as "What does each of you think?"

What are the downsides to using "I"? Underuse it, and you will be perceived as presumptive or wishy-washy. Overuse it in any group setting, and you run the risk of coming across as narcissistic, isolated, or arrogant.

More Refinements

Your choice of language means a lot to the people around you. As much as you might believe to the contrary, no one can read your mind. If you have a particular perspective or vision, you might assume that other people think the same way as you. Why wouldn't they? Invariably you discover this is not the case. Those around you have different values, knowledge, and experience. Your boss, your peers, and your team might have quite different ideas. It is your verbal and written language that lets people know what you want to happen.

In this next section, I will point out more language traps to avoid and provide specific ways to use language to empower people and get them excited.

Greetings Matter

Beginning a meeting or presentation with "Hello, everyone" includes everyone present. "Hello, New York" includes each person who aligns with being a New Yorker. Kennedy's 1963 greeting *"Ich bin ein Berliner"*(I am a Berliner) sent the message "I am with you, people of Berlin." Kennedy's statement was powerful because he identified himself with Berliners rather than expecting them to align with him.

Most languages have words for including everyone. Including greetings in the language of those present generates two things: a sense of belonging and a feeling of being valued. Each person there knows you are speaking to them, both individually and as a group.

The Language of Anonymity—It

The opposite of differentiating yourself is to make yourself anonymous. Leaders who want to hide use the word "it." So in this section, I want to talk about *it*—more specifically, the use of the pronoun "it."

"It" doesn't refer to anything or anyone in particular. The word is abstract and ambiguous. One of my mentors would say to me, "You can put 'it' in a wheelbarrow and wheel it around, but you still won't know what 'it' is! Define what 'it' is, and your audience will stay alongside you and understand."

CASE STUDY—TIM AND HIS LEADERSHIP TEAM

Tim's organization was facing significant public criticism of their handling of an incident, and he was preparing to talk with his team. Tim said, "It's a bad situation, and it isn't going away. It's affecting our ability to focus on our work. What are we going to do about it?"

I stopped him there and repeated his words, mirroring some of his fluster.

"That doesn't really nail what I want to say, does it?" Tim responded.

"Listening to you, I think there is a translation. I encourage you to identify each 'it.'"

Tim took a break to compose his thoughts. His next attempt was much better:

"Our approach to the current criticism isn't helpful to our progress. I realize the complaints are not going away, but they're taking attention away from what we need to get done. How do we want to respond?" Tim then gave his team a direction. "As we respond to each criticism, I want us to hold to our commitment to transparency and respect confidentiality. What goals do we want to achieve? How might we do this?"

Tim defines "it" as

- The current situation.
- The criticism.
- The effect of the criticisms.

Each of these is distinctive. By taking the time to specify "it" to his team, Tim is more easily understood and colleagues know better how to respond and engage.

Nailing That Interview with "I"

If you are unaccustomed to speaking up for yourself, you might think using "I" is boastful and egotistical and that "you" is more humble and diffuse. You are afraid of hogging the spotlight. However, humility won't get you the job you want. Interviewers want to hear from YOU in job interviews. Generalities or concepts are not enough. Specifically, interviewers want to hear about

- Your leadership practice.
- Your approach to developing people.
- How you create inspired teams.
- How you manage performance.
- Your track record in producing results.
- Your approach in turning tough situations around.
- Moments of courage.

Using "I" emotionally attracts people who want to hear more from the genuine you. Some leaders avoid this and fear the intimacy of being known and sharing their vision.

CASE STUDY: DEB

I was helping Deb to prepare for an interview by role-playing and practicing some questions she might be asked. I noticed she persisted in saying "you" when talking about her own leadership approach to specific situations.

I asked another practice question: "How do you respond to criticism?"

Deb responded, "You expect criticism in a job like this. You go about your everyday work, and you hear moans and groans. You just get used to it as part of your job. You can use criticism as part of a continuous improvement process."

Of course, I knew Deb was talking about herself, but I felt confused. Was she making a general statement on how people respond to criticism, or was she talking about me? I let her know what I was thinking. In an interview, interviewers want to get to know "you" and your leadership practice. They want to know how *you* respond when you are criticized, not some anonymous idea. By using "I," you can better convey your personality and approach to business.

I call this taking ownership of your leadership practice.

I suggested this and Deb took a second try. "I expect criticism in a job like mine. I go about my everyday work, and I hear moans and groans. I see addressing criticisms and concerns as part of my job. I listen and address everyone directly, and from time to time, I raise certain themes or concerns in team meetings. As a group, we work out interpersonal issues and make adjustments to our systems."

Deb's response gave me confidence that she listens and acts on her observations. I understood how she responds to criticism. Her interviewers would gain a clear sense of her leadership practice and be more likely to engage with her.

Where do we learn to hide ourselves in a group? As children, we are taught not to say "I" or to "show off." We are discouraged from expressing our childlike egotistical nature. As a leader, you are required to show your leader self, not your ego self.

Choose Verbs Wisely
Your choice of verb alongside your personal pronoun suggests significantly different intentions.
"I want . . ." creates inspiration. Here, want is an invitation.
"I need . . ." creates obligation. Need indicates a requirement.

CASE STUDY: JORGE

Jorge was about to enter into a performance discussion with one of his team managers. He had done a lot of background work, seeking feedback and actively reflecting on it. He had written his comments relating to the manager's objectives and wanted my perspective. I read over last few lines of his meeting notes: "You need to lead your team more, you need to delegate more, and you need to coach each team member."

I imagined each of these was a valid comment, but I noticed Jorge avoided giving his own view on the manager's effectiveness. I suggested that he include his thoughts on what he wanted the manager to develop. He began, "I like how you are managing me. You are keeping me updated on your results. You have good relationships with your key stakeholders. And I see you are motivated. And this quarter, I need you to expand what you are doing. You need to lead your team more, you need to delegate more, and you need to coach each team member . . ."

When I heard this, I sensed Jorge was desperate and frustrated. I asked him if this was the case. "Yes," he said, "I can see what he needs to do. How on earth do I communicate that?"

I noticed Jorge's emotional tone was negative. He sounded pressured. I repeated his words back to him—"I need you to . . . ," then asked, "What does that sound like?"

"That sounds as though what I am asking for is a requirement. As if what he does will benefit me in some way. It sounds like there will be consequences if he doesn't do this. How on earth do I shift the ownership to my team member?" Jorge sighed and continued, "I want him to succeed. I want him to be far more effective with his team."

Jorge worked out how he might inspire his team member to develop his abilities. His next draft was much better: "I want you to be an even more effective leader. I want you to actively lead your team, I want you to delegate more, and I want you to actively coach each team member to develop their abilities."

Where he had written "You should delegate more, and you should set priorities" he wrote "I want you to delegate more, and I want you to set priorities and work to these." Jorge and I reflected together. By using "I" rather than "you" in these examples and "want" rather than "need," Jorge was taking ownership of the direction he wanted his manager to develop and the results he wanted.

Jorge had shifted his language to be inviting and inspiring rather than demanding. He sounded engaged as he practiced, and his emotional tone was positive. The manager would be less likely to feel criticized and more likely to improve his abilities. I was confident he would sense Jorge's interest in his development.

Practice Session 9.1

Practice this with peers. Consider these examples of leaders using "we," "you," and "I." Are you included or excluded, being given a direction or being told what to do? Which do you find most engaging?

> *We need to focus on our strategic priorities . . .*
>
> *You need to focus on your strategic priorities . . .*
>
> *I want us to focus on our strategic priorities . . .*

Which of the three directions below leave you free to act?

> *"You need to practice 'I' statements this week."*
>
> *"I need you to practice 'I' statements this week."*
>
> *"I want you to practice 'I' statements this week."*

Practice Session 9.2: Upsides and Downsides of Communication

1. What's your positive relationship message in e-mails?
2. What is your positive relationship message when you begin talking with groups?

3. Which of the descriptions below do you identify with when under pressure?

   - Leaders who attend to relationship messages are seen as empathetic and approachable.

   - Leaders who overlook relationship messages are perceived as demanding, abrupt, or confrontational.

   - Leaders who overemphasize relationship messages are seen as people pleasers, soft, or wishy-washy.

   - Leaders who attend to their words are seen as clear, direct, and easy to understand.

   - Leaders who waffle, overexplain, and elaborate are perceived as boring, defensive, and irrelevant.

Summary

- Choosing your language wisely directly impacts your influence and success.

- Learning the personal and active language of leadership enhances your presence.

- Leaders learning the language of engagement impact their companies' bottom line.

- Leaders create unity of purpose by providing direction.

- Personal language creates immediacy, bringing everyone into the here and now.

- Discrimination in using "I," "you," and "we" gives leaders a powerful vocabulary with which to engage others.

Chapter 10

Powering Away from the Usual Suspects to Inspiring Others

I HAVE DISCOVERED THAT INSPIRING LEADERS create *genuine peer interactions*. In the final chapter, we will review how to take ownership of your own personal and professional development. We will recap ways to expand your capacities and learn fresh approaches to future dilemmas.

In Praise of Peer Relationships

In a peer relationship, neither of you acts superior or inferior to the other. You behave as respectful equals, regardless of hierarchical position or specialist identity.

You honestly say what you think and how you feel without second-guessing yourself or walking on eggshells. In such a positive mutual relationship, you expect comments to be received with goodwill. Misunderstandings are inevitable, but they are rapidly sorted out.

What could go wrong? Many things: Key players leave, organizational politics shift, fiscal pressures take their toll. Simply put, priorities change. Whatever it is, as you become more experienced in your organization, your relationship with authority figures will change and previous approaches may no longer work. From here on, it is your mandate to deal with difficult situations. Never assume things will get easier.

Leaders' capacities to give free and frank advice and have effective relationships with political representatives are frequently areas for their development. It is not the giving of free and frank advice that is problematic—it is giving the advice *and* maintaining the relationship. Positional power imbalances—and bosses and politicians who are aggressive, stressed, or disinterested—provide challenges for any leader to remain calm and engaged. Leaders' own values hold the key to deciding their approach. The lines they cross in these interactions are their own. Two repetitive patterns are evident: 1) They have come up against a familial or community value of equating "respect" with "being polite" to those more senior to you. 2) A treasured teacher has taught them particular social values that are irrelevant to their current situation. Rejecting the values is entangled with rejecting the treasured teacher. By asking themselves, What is the most important thing here? The outcome being sought, my feelings, or something else? Which of my values is being transgressed? Am I able to expand my values?" "What outcome would I want to function well in these settings?"

Your original family structure is a rich source of leadership material for exploring and developing peer relationships with those in authority over you. Many leaders laugh as they discover they are reenacting the role they had in their original family—be it the outlier, the family clown, Mom's or Dad's favorite, the fiercely independent one, the mediator, or the responsible one. They recognize that bosses and dysfunctional team members might well be unconsciously yet inevitably replicating dynamics from their own early family life.

There are several guidelines for having fruitful peer relationships. (1) Be a trusted confidant. (2) Be guided by trusted confidants. (3) Mirror and double your peers. (4) Never coach anyone unless they invite you to do so. Then think twice. Unless the coaching relationship is mutual, it won't work. If one of you becomes "the expert" and the other "the recipient," it is a recipe for disaster. (5) Be known for positive mutual relationships and having capacities for being influential even in stressful situations.

A Source of Glitches

When you find you are losing confidence in your capacity to have mutually positive relationships, or if you falter when with peers, seniors, or experts—the territory for your development has been revealed.

Each time you are anxious or frustrated with those in structural authority over you, or find yourself hesitant, frozen, or aggressive, your influence decreases. Whenever I ask a leader why they lose confidence, their responses invariably relate to some element of their original family dynamic. They unconsciously tap into default responses emanating from their early life.

Does this mean you have to trawl through your background to dig up moments you have carefully hidden or locked up? No. But reflecting on your background will reveal the setting where the current ineffective behavior or thinking originated. Then it is possible to examine the relationship between then and now. From there, the best approach depends on how you learn.

1. Be open to the idea that early life events influence your current responses.
2. Refer to a specific moment or event.
3. Represent the moment by using physical objects (such as pens, people, or a chair). Talk with the chosen object from your current experience and insight(s).
4. Accept the link and then focus on the here and now. How would you want to respond in this moment? What do you want to create now? What are the possibilities?
5. Determine the relevance of your habitual response to the current situation. If it is no longer relevant, cut the tie between the two events.
6. Place six objects on the floor between the original event and now. Assign each one a significant success you have had since the original event. Stock take afresh.

Each method is effective. Which one you choose depends on your preferred learning approach.

Ancient ruins have appeal for a reason. The Coliseum in Rome, the Marble Street of Ephesus, and the Egyptian pyramids have attracted millions of visitors over thousands of years. By imagining what was there, hearing the stories, marveling at the structures, and pondering the many lives lived, we understand something of ourselves. If you accept the people and events that have influenced you, your own capacity to influence will increase.

Coaches, too, have a moment of choice. They can teach basic techniques such as stress management, breathing, maintaining eye contact, or good posture. Or they can work on a deeper level by asking one of these questions:

- *How come you respond in this way?*
- *Where did you learn this?*
- *Who does this remind you of?*
- *Where else have you felt like this?*

Discovering originating events reveals leaders own forgotten stories. Some early influence helped shape you into the leader you are now, and yet it is no longer helpful. Leaders' overdeveloped behaviors have led them to become inflexible. By playing the role of *detective*, leaders can discover the provenance of their particular behaviors. They alone become accountable for how they want to respond *now*.

And here the coach and the leader arrive at a decision—how to proceed? Leaders respond in a variety of ways at this point. Most are relieved after realizing the connection. Some want to dive into unpacking what occurred in past; others prefer to cut the ties completely and leverage existing capacities and relationships. Still others move forward and search for new options that align with their values as a leader. This choice is up to the leader themselves. Each approach works.

What are the options for generating fresh approaches? There are several:

- Stimulate your imagination by seeing how others respond in similar situations.
- Imagine wild new strategies (not necessarily for use in real life!).
- Choose a path that strengthens the genuine you.

What Are Typical Overdeveloped Default Behaviors?

What are signs of overdeveloped default behaviors you and others might find? The usual suspects are:

- Inability to be clear and concise
- Bluntness to the point of being rude
- Worry about hurting others with what you have to say
- Overfamiliarity with others or cold withdrawal from people
- Failure to get the jobs you want
- Defensiveness, criticism, blaming, and judgment
- Silence on important matters
- Avoidance of sorting out interpersonal and intergroup conflicts
- Anxiety or aggression felt toward senior managers
- Isolation from your bosses, peers, or staff
- Reluctance to ask for what you want

When you recognize how you impact others, you begin a primary learning process. There are no predetermined recipes. The process is illogical, but it works. By opening up to fresh approaches aligned with your development outcomes, early wins are likely.

Yes, Two Worlds at the Same Time

Being present means living in at least two *worlds* at the same time: First, there is your responsive inner world, the intrapsychic world; second, there is the world of external relationships and interactions. Leaders can shift from being self-centered and focused on what others think of them to being people-centered and purposeful with those they lead. Their presence is determined by their choice of what is central to them at a given moment: either themselves and how they feel or their purpose with those around them.

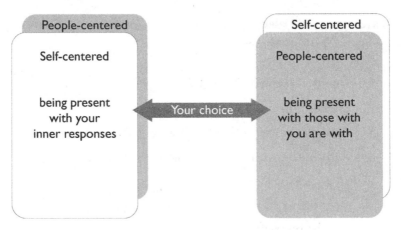

FIGURE 10.1 Being Present with Others

Find Cause, Not Blame

Our only reason for examining earlier life is to establish cause. Knowledge of the origin of default behavior allows leaders to act freely when under pressure. A truly fit-for-purpose response is fit for the leader's genuine self and fit for the context. Moreover, establishing cause enables leaders to remain accountable and intentional as they continue to learn and develop.

Intimacy comes from accepting the influence of significant others, identifying cause, and then taking responsibility for action. Bosses, staff, and colleagues are attracted to these leaders and are inspired by seeing them learn new responses.

Where leaders assign blame, most tend to enact short-term and formulaic solutions. Leaders who blame others for their own behavior tend to expect others to fix things. They cannot understand why things keep going wrong and regard their behavior as beyond their control. "But that is just me!" Because they don't *own* their development outcomes, they remain isolated from others and impervious to their perceptions.

Relying on techniques can be helpful in the short term, but behavioral learning is complex and takes time. Frequently the relief leaders feel after establishing the cause gives them the motivation to traverse the up-and-down terrain of practice and learning.

Taking responsibility creates heartache for leaders. Some will ask, "Why am I the one who has to raise this? Why doesn't anyone else notice what's going on?" The reason why is because you are the one who cares. You will recognize this feeling yourself.

Some Relationships Don't Work

At some point in our lives, we all have made poor choices of partners, friends, bosses, and staff. Relationships that begin with high hopes often end in disappointment, betrayal, and rejection. This is normal. What isn't normal is when poor choices continue as a pattern. If you start looking for a common thread, you may be surprised to discover it is *you*. "Before you accuse me, take a look at yourself"—words of wisdom from Eric Clapton.

With this in mind, you can choose your response when you are rejected. Realize you have made a relationship mistake, and recognize that you will inevitably have an emotional response. Work rejections take several forms:

- Not being chosen for a project you wanted
- Being excluded from an important meeting
- Being laid off
- Losing control of your project to another
- Being ignored by your boss

- Getting a poor review from your boss

Actually, these are not rejections. They may feel like rejections or betrayals, but these result from misunderstanding, or poor communication, or someone being chosen as first preference while you might be the second or third choice.

Not being appointed to a role you want can feel like rejection. It is not. The interviewers preferred another candidate based on criteria unknown to you. Don't take this personally unless missing out on being appointed is persistent and repetitive.

When your feelings have abated—and you can think clearly—focus on what is important to you. Holding on to your hurts and resentments or being the *dedicated savior* or *optimistic magician* for others won't help here.

Knowing when to say no, cut yourself loose, terminate someone's employment, or turn a relationship around is precisely leaders' territory. Whatever option is chosen, being purposeful and retaining respectful relationships is the desired outcome.

Two criteria assist in making decisions regarding rejection: *liking* and *respect*. If your decisions are based on wanting to be *liked*, your judgment will be clouded. If your decisions are based on wanting to be *respected*, things are still tough, but easier.

CASE STUDY: DIANA

Like everyone else, I have had relationships where my overdeveloped default behaviors became active. After working closely for some years, a peer let me down badly. I became critical of him, and we sparred constantly and upset those close to both of us. I felt disregarded by him, while he felt (and was) criticized by me. We both discussed who we reminded one another of, which led to some clarity but did little to improve our relationship.

Unable to make a shift in my response, I consulted with my professional development supervisor. He suggested I make two columns on a page, and write the name of my peer and the sibling he reminded me of at the top of each column and note the similarities between them. I did so and found there were eighteen. Then I noted the differences. After three or four, it dawned on me I was responding in a way I wished I had when I was younger. I knew my current response no longer worked. Over time, the sting in our relationship lessened. Both of us chose not to work with one another, although we remain professional peers.

Discovering a Behavioral Glitch

After discovering your faulty behaviors, there are at least five options available:

- Ignore it and hope it goes away. *While this seems simple, it rarely works. You'll find yourself making excuses, mulling it over, and analyzing why it happened and what the other players were doing. You are likely to notice each time the behavior manifests. All these reactions are time consuming and emotionally draining.*
- Pretend it's insignificant. *As above, if you care about your work and the people you trust, uncovering a glitch is significant.*
- Learn a technique to get by. *This is a short-term approach. This will give you time to consult with significant others and decide what you want to do, if anything.*
- Apologize each time. *Habitual or repetitive apologizing is a social behavior that doesn't fix the root problem.*
- Discover what the glitch is and where it came from. Break the link and develop a fresh approach.

The first four gain you time and space. Option five strengthens your presence. If you consistently disappoint or upset the people you serve, they move away psychologically. You know you have missed the mark and that your response is unhelpful. You habitually shut things down. Why does that happen? See this as an opportunity to expand your capacities, keep learning, and try a fresh approach.

As we have seen, leaders need courage to accept their imperfections. Accept that minor changes will have significant impacts, and that making psychological and emotional shifts will open a pathway forward. Reliving old memories can be unpleasant, but it is better than knowing you could be more effective yet are unwilling to try.

Most leaders I know want to do a good job, yet some unspoken feeling holds them back or skews their actions. Everyone I know has one or more of the following private fears and anxieties to some degree:

- Fear of failure
- Fear of not being liked or accepted
- Fear of not being up to it
- Fear of rejection
- Fear of being criticized or judged
- Fear of standing alone
- Fear of speaking up
- Fear of hurting someone
- Fear of not knowing what to do
- Fear of making mistakes

Now that is a lot of fears. Fear is a normal and inevitable emotion. The role of fear is to help us make wise decisions. It is a reactive response to what motivates you and what you want to create in the world. Typically, leaders are motivated to

- Improve people's lives
- Do a good job
- Solve significant social, economic, environmental, or business problems
- Have great relationships
- Run successful organizations people love to work in

- Make a profit by providing great services
- Make a contribution to the world

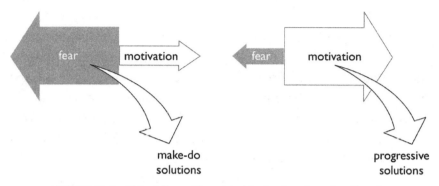

FIGURE 10.2   When Fears Override Motivation, Inaction Results

When leaders' fears loom larger than their motivations, they become risk averse or procrastinate. This results in inaction or restrictive solutions. By working with their fears, leaders can generate progressive behavior.[1]

The addiction recovery movement has a working acronym for fear: **False Evidence Appearing Real.** When they remain private or unconscious, their fears will cause leaders to behave in ways that are

- Risk averse
- Overly helpful
- Perfectionistic
- Silent
- Frozen
- Tentative
- Combative
- Agitated

---

[1] Our model is based on the focal conflict model of Dorothy Stock Whitaker and Morton A. Lieberman.

What helps is letting people know your fears: "This scares the bejesus out of me, and I have no idea what to do. Here's where we want to end up. Let's hear your thoughts. What are our options?" What helps is data and information. What helps is finding out the full picture. What helps is asking, "What is the worst that can happen?"

Whenever people reveal their fears, know you can help. You can accept their anxiety and help expand their perceptions with ordinary everyday information. The reality is that when we disregard fear, we pull back and charge ahead at the same time. We fail to use what we know as leaders.

For years, I have listened to leaders who hesitated before taking action or speaking honestly because they feared losing their jobs or important relationships. However, most jobs are lost because of restructures or shifts in business direction—things out of their control. Leaders who know they are effective know they will find another job, one even better than what they currently have. If you fear losing your job, make sure your CV is compelling and up to date.

You Are the Boss

My best advice is to take ownership of your own leadership development. Listen carefully to significant others before deciding your own development outcomes. That will give you the best results. Give yourself time to develop new capacities, rather than expecting immediate results. By defining what success looks like for you, you can choose indicators that will help you to effectively track your progress.

By giving yourself plenty of room to learn, you will see your patterns of behavior and assess what works and what doesn't. You can create your own three-year plan. Here's a list of useful areas of development you might choose to explore:

- Read people and respond relevantly.
- Read situations rapidly.
- Develop trusted peer relationships rapidly.
- Trust your intuition, judgment, and perceptions.

- Learn to collaborate.
- Stop being defensive; be responsive.
- Be an authority without being authoritarian.
- Be direct and say what you want to say while retaining relationships.
- Share your vision, inspire others, and deliver results.
- Enjoy your abilities while staying open to expanding your capacities.

How do you know where to begin? There is no best place to begin. What is best is to choose one that really appeals to you, let people know what you are learning, and practice. Executive presence is not about future proofing; it is about being human, being genuine and visionary in your relationships, and creating positive futures for others and yourself.

Practice Session 10.1

Identify six things you have learned in the past year which have assisted you to achieve better results.

1. _____
2. _____
3. _____
4. _____
5. _____
6. _____

Practice Session 10.2

From page 200–201, write one development outcome for yourself for this next year.

Practice session 10.3

- What fears drive your behavior?
- What is your motivating force with each one?

- Who would know you have these fears?
- What is the worst thing that could happen?
- Where has this fear come from?
- What facts and information would allay these fears?
- What practical actions can you take to mitigate your fears?

Practice Session 10.4

What is your story? Write your story down on a page.

- What have you learned from this experience?
- What in this story helps you lead?
- What in this story has held you back?

Summary

- Peer relationships are equal regardless of hierarchical position.
- Recognition of how you impact others begins a holistic learning process.
- Your presence is determined by your choice of where your focus is along a continuum: on yourself and those you lead.
- Finding the cause of default behaviors gives you freedom to decide what areas you want to develop, how you will do so, and whom you want to help.
- Take ownership of your own leadership development.

Bibliography

Adkins, Amy. "Only 35% of U.S. Managers Are Engaged in Their Jobs." *Gallup Business Journal*, April 2, 2015, http://www.gallup.com/businessjournal/182228/managers-engaged-jobs.aspx.

Albrecht, Karl. *Social Intelligence: The New Science of Success.* New York: Pfeiffer, 2009.

Australian and Aotearoa New Zealand Psychodrama Association. http://aanzpa.org.

Barsade, Sigal, and Olivia O'Neill. "Manage Your Emotional Culture," *Harvard Business Review*, January–February 2016, https://hbr.org/2016/01/manage-your-emotional-culture.

Buckingham, Marcus, and Ashley Goodall. "Reinventing Performance Management," *Harvard Business Review*, April 2015, https://hbr.org/2015/04/reinventing-performance-management.

Clayton, Lynette. "The Use of the Cultural Atom to Record Personality Changes in Individual Psychotherapy," *Journal of Group Psychotherapy, Psychodrama and Sociometry* (35): 111–117.

Clayton, Max. "The Preparation and Writing of a Social and Cultural Atom Paper," *AANZPA* 4 (December 1995): 43–50.

Clayton, G. M. *Living Pictures of the Self.* Caulfield, Australia: ICA Press, 1993.

Freud, Sigmund. *Group Psychology and the Analysis of the Ego.* New York, Boni and Liveright. 1922

Gladwell, Malcolm. *Blink: The Power of Thinking without Thinking.* New York: Little, Brown and Company, 2005.

Goldsmith, Marshall. *Triggers: Creating Behavior That Lasts.* New York: Crown Business, 2015.

Goleman, Daniel. *Emotional Intelligence: Why It Can Matter More than IQ.* New York: Bantam Books, 2005.

Gurdjian, Pierre, Thomas Halbeisen, and Kevin Lane. "Why Leadership-Development Programs Fail." *McKinsey Quarterly*, January 2014, www.mckinsey.com/global-themes/leadership/why-leadership-development-programs-fail.

Hale, Ann. *Conducting Clinical Sociometric Explorations.* Roanoke, VA: Royal Publishing Company, 1985.

Hale, Ann E. *Three Cyclical Models Which Enhance Consciousness of Interpersonal Connections,* International Sociometry Training network, 2012.

Hay Group, "Insight to Impact: Leadership That Gets Results," pamphlet, www.haygroup.com/us/downloads, last accessed 2016.

Horney, Karen. *Our Inner Conflicts: A Constructive Theory of Neurosis.* London: Routledge, 1946.

Howie, Peter, and Elizabeth Synnot. "Levels of Learning." ANZPA white paper, January 2006, www.moreno.com.au/levels-learning-model -peter-howie-and-elizabeth-synnot.

Jones, Diana. "The Way We Do Things around Here: The Role of Leadership Teams in Shaping Progressive Organizational Cultures." *Australian and Aotearoa New Zealand Psychodrama Association* 21 (2012): 53–63.

Mankins, Michael C. "Stop Wasting Valuable Time," *Harvard Business Review,* September 2004, https://hbr.org/2004/09/stop-wasting-valuable-time.

"Mehrabian's Communication Research," BusinessBalls. www.businessballs .com/mehrabiancommunications.htm.

Mehrabian, Albert. *Silent Messages: Implicit Communication of Emotions and Attitudes.* Belmont, CA: Wadsworth, 1981.

Milgram, Stanley. *Obedience to Authority: An Experimental View.* New York: HarperCollins, 2004.

Moreno, Jacob. *Sociometry and the Cultural Order.* New York: Beacon House, 1943.

Moreno, Jacob. *Who Shall Survive?* New York: Beacon House, 1953.

Moreno, Zerka. *Quintessential Zerka: Writings by Zerka Toeman Moreno on Psychodrama, Sociometry and Group Psychotherapy.* London: Routledge, 2015.

New Zealand State Services Commission. "Leadership Insight: Initial Findings." May 2016, www.ssc.govt.nz/sites/all/files/leadership-insight-findings -report-may16.pdf.

Petrie, Nick. *Future Trends in Leadership Development.* Center for Creative Leadership, white paper, 2014, www.ccl.org/wp-content/uploads/2015/04/ futureTrends.pdf.

Psychodrama Australia. www.psychodramaaustralia.com.

Radicati, Sara, and Justin Levenstein. *"Email Statistics Report"* 2013–2017.

Reilly, Robin. "Five Ways to Improve Employee Engagement Now." *Gallup Business Journal,* January 7, 2014, www.gallup.com/businessjournal/166667/ five-ways-improve-employee-engagement.aspx.

"Relationship and Content Messages," Conflict Management. www.conflict management.co.nz/relationship-and-content-messages.

Senge, Peter. *The Fifth Discipline: The Art and Practice of the Learning Organization*. New York: Doubleday, 2006.

Snipes, Jeff, and Jami York. "Leadership Development Practices of Top-Performing Organizations," Ninth House, March 10, 2006, www.cedma-europe.org/newsletter%20articles/KnowledgeAdvisors/KA0603/NinthHouseJeffSnipes.pdf.

Sperling, Julia and Schwartz, David. "Leadership and Behavior: Mastering the Mechanics of Reason and Emotion." *McKinsey Quarterly*, October 2016, http://www.mckinsey.com/business-functions/organization/our-insights/leadership-and-behavior-mastering-the-mechanics-of-reason-and-emotion.

Swink, David F. "Don't Type at Me Like That! Email and Emotions. Emails Have Feelings Too." *Psychology Today*, 2013.

Tabrizi, Behnam. "Collaboration: 75% of Cross-Functional Teams Are Dysfunctional." *Harvard Business Review*, June 23, 2015.

Weber, Max. *Rationalism and Modern Society*, edited and translated by Tony Waters and Dagmar Waters, New York: Palgrave Macmillan 2015.

Whitaker, D. S., and M. A. Lieberman. *Psychotherapy through the Group Process*. New York: Atherton; London: Tavistock, 1964.

Williams, Antony. *Forbidden Agendas: Strategic Action in Groups*. New York: Routledge, 1991.

Winter, Eyal. "Feeling Smart: Why Our Emotions Are More Rational Than We Think." *Public Affairs*, 2014.

Zenger, Jack, and Joe Folkman. "Do You Need to Lighten Up or Toughen Up?" *Harvard Business Review*, March 10, 2014, https://hbr.org/2014/03/do-you-need-to-lighten-up-or-toughen-up.

Zenger, Jack, and Joe Folkman. "Feedback: The Powerful Paradox." www.zengerfolkman.com/wp-content/uploads/2013/03/ZF-Feedback-The-Powerful-Paradox.pdf, 2014.

Index